CANNABIS GROWING GUIDE

INDOOR and OUTDOOR

How to Grow Healthy Marijuana Plants INDOOR and OUTDOOR for High Quality Medical Cannabis

Monica Jacobs

Table of Contents

Chapter 1: What is Cannabis?

In this chapter, we will look at the meaning of cannabis, the various chemicals that it contains and why growing your own plants is a great idea. Cannabis is an herb that has remained popular amongst medics since time immemorial. It contains chemicals beneficial for the entire body including blood, muscles, and bones and also skin.

Better known as marijuana amongst enthusiasts, the plant's seeds, leaves, and flowers are harvested for the medicinal benefits that they provide. As mentioned earlier, cannabis is a psychoactive, capable of altering a person's mindset. It is predominantly rolled into a joint and smoked to avail an outer worldly experience. The drug imparts its effect for 5 to 6 hours after consumption.

What's interesting is, people did not begin using the plant to avail its mind-altering effects for a long time since its discovery. It was mainly used to prepare medicines that helped in combating many illnesses and delaying their occurrences. We will shed light on some of these conditions in the last chapter of this book.

Cannabis can also be used in cooking. Right from curries to biscuits and cakes, it is possible to incorporate canna-oil and canna-butter and enhance its health benefits. Some people also add in powdered cannabis leaves to the dishes to avail its full medicinal benefits. We will look at basic canna-oil and cannabutter recipes later in this book.

Cannabis contains many chemicals that collectively make it an extremely potent drug. Despite containing hundreds of chemicals, only a few have been successfully identified. We will look at these chemicals in detail and understand why they are beneficial for your body.

Chemicals present in marijuana

THC

Tetrahydrocannabinol (THC for short) is the most widely present chemical in cannabis. Tetrahydrocannabinol makes up for about 9% of the overall chemical content in cannabis. THC binds with the cannabinoids in the central nervous system and enhances immunity while relaxing physical pain. This chemical, however, is not much sought after when it comes to preparing medicines. THC has the maximum psychoactive effects on the mind. Smokers interested in availing a good trip will always look for yields high in this chemical.

CBD

CBD stands for cannabidiol. It has almost no psychoactive effect thereby making it a much safer extract of the plant. Extensively used in the preparation of medicines, CBD is sought after by those that prepare traditional medicines. It is predominantly used in the preparation of anti-epileptic, anti-rheumatic and arthritis medicines. Research is still on to understand the full effects of this chemical on the body.

CBN

CBN or cannabinol is produced in the plant when the THC content is exposed to light. It has very little psychoactive and is mostly used in medicines. It is used for its anti-spasmodic and anti- epileptic effects. It also has a sedative effect on the mind.

Terpene

Terpene is the molecule that contains these chemicals. They are predominantly found in the leaves, buds, and flowers of the plant. The concentration of terpene depends on the quality and variety of the plant. The best quality plant will have a strong and pungent terpene while a weaker strain will have mild and sweeter terpene.

These are the well-known and well-researched chemicals present in cannabis. They are what have maximum medicinal properties.

Why grow your own cannabis?

Cannabis is illegal because of its potential of being abused. High tendency cannabis is capable of inducing an addiction if not smoked responsibly. Many governments have therefore banned the substances.

But it is fine to grow your own cannabis if you wish to put it to medicinal use.

Here are some of the reasons why you should grow your own cannabis.

Time saving

It is quite important for those depending on cannabis for health purposes to have some at their quick disposal. This is not possible if they rely on others to bring them the plant. The best thing in such a situation is to grow your own plants. It is quite easy to do so and will allow you to have plants all in different stages of growth.

Cost effective

Growing your own cannabis plants will ensure that you save on quite a bit of money on a monthly basis. You need not have to pay the dealer his fees. The cost per gram of the product will also considerably reduce.

Peace of mind

Growing your own cannabis plants will ensure that you remain with a peaceful mind. Forget having to contact a dealer and going through all of that hassle. All you will have to do is walk over to your balcony or growing room and snip off some fresh plant to decarboxylate and start using. You do not have to worry about getting caught for it.

Consistency

Growing your own cannabis plants will ensure you remain with a consistent supply of the weed. Having different plants growing in different stages can help in remaining with enough cannabis at all times.

Control

Growing your own plants will allow you to exercise control over its quality. You might not have the same control over whatever cannabis is given to you by the dealer. It will be possible for you to enhance the quality output of the plant by using good quality fertilizers and remain with good yield.

NOTE: Growing your own cannabis means you will have easy access to it and so must be cautious to use it responsibly.

What to expect after smoking/ consuming cannabis

Whether it is a strong strain or a weak one that you have consumed, cannabis can have one or all of the following effects on your body.

- You will instantly start feeling great about yourself! Cannabis increases the dopamine content in your brain thereby increasing the feeling of happiness. This can continue for some time, as the drug is bioavailable in the body for 5 to 6 hours.
- You will feel like all your aches and pains have disappeared. The herb has a numbing effect on the body thereby reducing the feeling of pain and uneasiness.
- You might suffer from short-term memory loss. This is completely fine, as the mind will be focusing on the release of serotonin and suppression of cortisol.
- If you were feeling sick before smoking up then the feeling will completely disappear as and when you start puffing. Cannabis helps in reducing nausea and combats vomiting sensation.
- Your eyes might dry out, and your skin might turn red. Better known as baking, the chemicals present in cannabis can impart a reddish glow to the skin thereby making you appear red.
- Cannabis is also an amazing muscle relaxant. You will feel at ease and not feel like moving a muscle.
- Some people feel drowsy after consuming cannabis. You might feel quite sleepy after smoking up, especially after smoking a potent strain.
- You might have dryness in your mouth for some time.

Long-term use

Long-term use of cannabis can have a few side effects, which are as follows

- Long-term use of cannabis can affect your heart health. You might be more prone to strokes and cardiovascular illnesses
- It can affect your lung health and cause the onset of asthma
- Long term use of cannabis also results in memory loss
- There are high chances of addiction if you do not smoke cannabis responsibly

It is, therefore, advisable to consume cannabis responsibly and treat as medicine.

Chapter 2: Things Required to Grow Cannabis Plants

It might seem a little daunting to take up such a venture but should not stop you from trying your hand at growing your own cannabis plants.

To help you get started on the right foot, here are some things that you have to arrange for before starting to grow your plants.

Basic requirements

Here is a list of basic things that you will require for your cannabis garden.

Buckets

Buckets are best to grow cannabis plants. They will be spacious enough to accommodate medium to large plants. Good quality plastic buckets are your best bet as they will be quite sturdy. Anywhere from 15 to 25 gallons are ideal for the job. Using a drill bit, drill enough holes at the bottom of the bucket to drain away excess water. It is also an option to make use of cement pots. They can hold a lot more soil and make for better options when it comes to growing cannabis plants indoors.

Soil

The soil required for the job should be of good quality. Organic soil is the best as it contains a lot of natural chemicals and elements that are vital for growing healthy cannabis plants. It is quite simple to make your own soil base by mixing equal parts red soil with black soil and fertilizers. This combination works well for all varieties of cannabis plants and encourages consistent growth. But remember to use loose soil capable of draining away excess liquid as water retention can lead to root damage.

Seeds/ grafts

When it comes to growing cannabis plants, both seeds and grafts work well. High quality seeds bought from reliable lenders will allow you to grow high quality plants. There are many seed varieties available and some of them are as follows.

- **Indica**: Indica seeds are predominantly medicinal seeds. They are impactful on the body but not so much on the mind. These are best to consider if you are looking to avail the plant's medicinal benefits.

- **Sativa**: Sativa strains have a strong THC content thereby making them potent psychoactive. These are grown to be smoked.

- **Hybrid**: Hybrids are a combination of Indica and Sativa. They will provide you with plants that have an equal effect on your mind and body.

- **Flowering**: The last is a flowering variety that produces potent flowers containing high concentrations of the chemical.

Consider growing plants using the different strains to know what works best for you.

Tools

You will require minimal tools when it comes to growing cannabis plants. A basic gardening kit including a spade and a rake will suffice. You will need a pair of shears and small precision scissors to trim the plants.

Nutrients

Soil tends to lose vital nutrients over a period of time thereby necessitating the addition of nutrient rich liquids. Pick the best ones available in the market and follow the instructions carefully. You have to be careful not to overfeed the plants as that can ruin them. Vermiculture is a great additive to work with while growing cannabis. With time, you will be able to come up with a winning formula that will work great with your plants.

Disease control

Cannabis plants are prone to certain diseases that can take over the entire plant in no time. It is best to make use of natural ingredients such as neem oil to control the onset and spread of illnesses.

Advanced requirements

Here are a few advanced items that you will require if you wish to grow the plants indoors.

Exhaust fans

Exhaust fans are a must to control the temperature in the room. They work by eliminating the hot air and encouraging the circulation of cool air. This is a vital part of growing plants indoors, as they require the perfect temperature to grow well.

Air conditioners

If the room is too hot for the plants then it is a must to install air conditioners. Cannabis plants like pleasant temperatures and will thrive in cold atmospheres. Regulating the temperature from time to time will ensure good growth and great yield.

Carbon Dioxide emitters

Carbon dioxide emitters can be set up close to the plants to help them grow well. Many people set it up to enhance the THC content of the plants. You will have two choices to pick from including propane based and tank based emitters. The former are cheaper and work better as compared to the latter.

Lighting

Every indoor system requires ample lighting. After all, the plants need enough light to make their food. In the absence of sunlight, cannabis plants thrive under LED grow lights or CFL bulbs. Setting up a cost effective system that concentrates plenty of light over the plants will ensure that you remain with a good yield.

Hydroponics

Those interested in doing away with soil can turn to hydroponics. Hydroponics makes use of water-based systems to encourage the growth of plants. Setting one up is quite simple and will only require assembling the system in the desired room. This method of growing is both cost effective and result in healthier plants.

Apart from these you will require some basic things such as gloves, baskets jars etc.

Once you have everything sorted you will be ready to begin gardening.

Chapter 3: Growing Cannabis Indoors

Growing cannabis plants indoors is a better option as compared to growing it outdoors. You will be able to grow them freely without having to worry about getting noticed by others.

Here are the steps to follow.

Growing site

The growing site will have to be picked carefully. The atmosphere in the room should be conducive for the plants. A small closet or cupboard will serve as an ideal site to grow the plants. There should be a window or vent to help hot air escape easily. If there is no such space available then grow tents make for a good option.

Temperature

The temperature in the room should be pleasant. Cannabis tends to wilt in very hot temperatures and grow slowly in cold ones. It is therefore essential to provide the plants with temperatures that encourage free growth. The ideal temperature to grow cannabis is between 62 and 80 degrees Fahrenheit.

Lights

Set up lights all around the plants. They will be replacing sunlight and should be available to the plant at all times. Arrange them in such a way that some lights remain above the plants and some on the sides. It will be easier for you to set it up in a grow tent.

Soil

Prepare your own soil mix by mixing together 2 parts red soil, 2 parts black soil and 2 parts vermiculture. This is a great mix to both start and grow your cannabis plants. If you don't have access to black soil then simply use 4 parts red soil.

Germinating

Germinating the seeds will ensure that the plants grow faster. The time taken for them to poke their heads out will be considerably lesser as compared to directly growing them in soil. To germinate them add about 10 to 12 seeds in separate starting mediums. Place them in a warm place and water regularly. In about a week's time the seeds will germinate. Do not try to remove the plants from the medium. They will have to be transplanted along with some of the medium.

Sowing

Add the soil mix about 3/4ths of the way in the pot. Make small holes, about 2 inches deep, in the soil and leave a gap of about 5 inches between each. Add in the saplings into the holes and cover gently. Water the plants immediately.

Water

Water cannabis plants every alternate day or wait until the topsoil dries out. Add the water in slowly and wait until all of it is completely absorbed. The water should reach the roots of the plant in order for them to grow well. Add some water from the top down, from time to time, to give the leaves a boost. But make sure that water does not remain on the leaves as that can lead to fungus formation.

Nutrients

It is very important to add a good amount of nutrients to the cannabis plants from time to time. It is obvious that soil will lose essential nutrients, which will have to be replaced. Pick something rich in phosphorous and potassium, as they will enhance plant growth. They will also improve the THC content in the plant.

Trimming

Trimming the plant from time to time will ensure proper growth. It will also pay to separate the male and female plants. Using sharp shears to cut away some of the initial growth will only lead to thicker and bushier plants. But be careful so as not to cut away too much as that can damage the plants.

Cannabis will be ready to harvest in about 2 months time. We will look at the harvesting process a little later in the book.

Chapter 4: Growing Cannabis Outdoors

Cannabis plants grow well outdoors just as they do indoors. Here is how to grow healthy plants outside your house.

Season

Spring is the best time to start growing your cannabis plants. They will thrive during this month and reach their peak during early summer. If there is danger of frost during winters then consider using heavy mulch to protect the roots of the plants.

Site selection

The very next step is to select an appropriate site to sow the seeds. Basically, you need to look for one that humans and animals cannot easily access. Although your backyard is a good place, your terrace might make for a better bet. It should have sufficient natural light coming through and remain close to a water source. All of these elements are collectively essential when looking for the best site to start growing your cannabis plants and a little care goes a long way in growing healthy strains.

Preparing the site

Next, prepare the site by clearing away all the weed and stray plants that are growing in the soil. Remove big rocks and stones that might present on the top surface. Using a plough make 10 to 12 holes in the soil at about 4 feet space each. Make them 2 feet deep, as that would be ideal to sow the seeds.

Germinating

Next, you have to germinate the seeds. Seeds can take around 2 weeks to germinate. Remember that the black ones will germinate as compared to the white ones. Sow them in coco coir or any starting medium and water on alternate days. Soaking the seeds in a little water for a couple of days will help them sprout. Ones the tiny heads start to poke out, they will be ready to transfer to a permanent place.

Pots

If you are growing the plants in pots then start by adding good quality soil to it. Pat it down and add in a layer of fertilizer. Make three to four holes in the soil to place the saplings.

Sowing

Carefully transfer the saplings to the holes and cover them gently. You might have to make use of light fingers to spread the soil around the plant. Pat it down and water immediately.

Sunlight

Cannabis plants require a minimum of 4 hours direct sun to thrive. More is always good and will result in healthier plants. If the sun is too harsh then consider covering the plant until nighttime. They will grow much faster in summer as compared to winter.

Water

Cannabis plants do not require too much water to thrive. Watering them on alternate days will help in remaining with a good yield. Over watering will result in root and leaf damage. Water as soon as the topsoil dries out. Ensure to add in nutrient rich liquids every 3 weeks to keep up the health of the soil.

Grafting

Sowing grafts is much simpler as compared to growing plants from seeds. All you have to do is place the graft in the appropriate area and gently cover the area around it with soil. Water it as you would water your saplings and the cannabis plant will begin to thrive.

Trimming

Trim the plants every so often to ensure that they are not fighting for space. An important aspect to consider here is that it is essential to remove and discard the male plants. Male plants do not produce strong leaves and buds. They will only pollinate the female plants and affect their output. The best way to tell between male and female plants is look at their buds. The male plants will have small round, green buds whereas female plants carry stigmas.

Cannabis plants can take anywhere between a month to two months to produce flowers. You have to remain patient until such time and can then begin to harvest the crop.

Chapter 5: Cannabis Harvesting Drying and Curing Guide

Like most other plants, it is important to harvest cannabis on time, to ensure the maintenance of its cannabinoid content.

Harvesting the plant too soon can result in the loss of important THC and CBD content. You surely do not want to remain with a crop whose molecules have degraded.
Similarly, harvesting it too late can result in the disintegration of the CBD and CBN content, which again will result in a poor crop.

It is therefore vital to know exactly when to harvest your plants so that you remain with the best yield.

THC is mostly present in the leaves and buds all through the growing phase of the plant. However, it only starts to develop around the buds during harvest season.
This makes it all the more important to pluck the buds in time, in order to avail a crop rich in THC, CBD and CBN.

If you wait too long after the chemical has remained on the bud, and then you will be left with a plant that is too strong and capable of inducing nausea.

Here are some tips for you to know exactly when to pluck the buds from the plant.

THC to CBD

For those looking to avail the medicinal effects of the plant, it is best to wait for some of the THC to convert into CBD. CBD is the chemical that is extensively used in the preparation of medicines and so; waiting for it to rise in content will leave you with a stronger crop.

Signs of plant maturity

There are many signs to look for when it comes to harvesting cannabis. The plant will start to take shape and giveaway signals that it is ready to be plucked, dried and cured. Here is looking at some of the major signs.

- When the plant is approaching maturity, the flowers will merge with each other and the ovaries will swell up. Tiny pink crystals can be noticed around the flowers, which contain the vital chemicals
- Some of the plant's leaves will start to darken and wilt. This is a good way to tell that the plant is almost ready to harvest
- The trichomes are what will give away the final signals. Trichomes are small structures present on the leaves and flowers. They are rich in THC content and will help in knowing exactly when the leaves and buds can be plucked
- Signs to check with the trichomes include the flattening of the heads into a mushroom shape, a change in their color (white to cloudy) and finally, the go from cloudy to brown
- When the trichomes are cloudy, they will contain maximum THC content. If you are looking to avail a strong narcotic effect then this is the best time to harvest it. Once they turn dark brown, the CBD content reaches its peak. This is a great time to harvest to avail its medicinal properties

Harvesting cannabis

Harvesting cannabis is pretty straightforward and here are the different steps to follow.

- Start by removing all the large leaves of the plant. These are the fan shaped ones that grow all over the plant
- Next, remove the smaller leaves on the plant. Some people leave them on in order to harvest a strong crop later on
- Make use of sharp scissors to individually cut out the buds and kolas. Do not lose patience and chop off entire sections of the plant as that will not yield a good crop
- Make use of secateurs to cut off the stems from the plant. If you missed removing any the large leaves at the beginning then now is a good time to do the needful
- Do not pile them up on top of each other as that can damage the vital buds

Drying cannabis

It is no secret that cannabis comes in many varieties and flavors. The terpenes in each plant are different and will lend the bud a unique flavor.

Here is looking at the steps that will help you dry your buds in the correct manner.

- The very first step is to prepare the drying area. Your drying area should be clean and provide for plenty of fresh air to circulate within the room. Ensure that the temperature inside the room is pleasant enough for each and every plant to dry equally

- If you are keen on drying the plants in a heat box then consider preparing one using cardboards. Look up instructions on the internet for the same
- Once the room is ready, hang the cannabis plants one by one. Allow enough room between them to allow air circulation
- The average drying time for cannabis plants is 1 week. This can vary depending on the variety
- The best way to check whether your plant has successfully dried up is to lightly bend the stem. If it cracks then the plant has successfully dried. If it remains firm then it is better to give it some more time

Cleaning and curing cannabis

- Once the buds have completely dried, it is time to give them a trim. Making use a sharp precision scissor, cut away any of the remaining leaves that enclose the buds. This is an important step of the process, as the leaves can cause the buds to fall off
- Once done, the buds will be ready to be cured. Prepare enough glass jars by sterilizing them to cure the buds. Although you have the option of using plastic jars, it is preferable to use glass, as it will help the buds dry out faster
- Fill in each glass with just the buds after carefully cutting them out using the precision scissors
- Close the lid and store the jar in a dark place. Make use of airtight jars, as oxygen can speed up plant aging
- You have to remove the lid for 15 minutes on a daily basis to help the buds breathe
- Your buds will be ready in a week or so. Leaving them in the jar for longer will yield a stronger crop

Storage

Storing cannabis is pretty easy. Leaving them in the same jars that were used to cure them will ensure that you keep the buds fresh for long. You can also vacuum seal the dried leaves. All you have to do is add it to a Ziploc bag and suck out the air from it. This will keep the herb fresh for long and provide great medicinal benefits.

If in case you have harvested a lot of buds and don't wish to dry all of them then you can always freeze the spare. Wrap it in brown paper and stick it into the freezer to preserve it. Once you are ready to dry them, allow the plants to thaw for sometime before hanging them in the hanging room.

Chapter 6: Tips to Grow Healthy Plants

Cannabis plants are pretty hardy and grow in a variety of conditions. However, only the best maintained plants would give away quality yield.

Here is looking at some tips to enhance the overall health of your cannabis plants.

Flushing the plant

Flushing your plants just before harvesting them will ensure a stronger yield. Flushing is the simple process of providing your plants with plain water as compared to nutrient rich water. If they are accustomed to receiving water containing added nutrients, then it is best to give them plain water during harvest season. It will boost plant health and leave you with higher levels of THC. However, there is a flipside to watch out for! Over watering your plants at this stage can potentially risk the health of your precious buds and cause them to fall out prematurely. You have to therefore remain careful and wait for the topsoil to dry out before watering your plants. If you don't want to take a risk with tap water then can settle for pH balanced water available online. This water will ensure the pH level in the soil remains at a certain ideal level.

Variety

One great trick to remain with quality yield is to make use of a diverse range of seeds. By planting seeds that fall into a wide genetic range, you will successfully remain with a better crop. For this, collect seeds from different, healthy, strains and pool them together. Randomly plant all of them in the pots to ensure that each one gives away a healthy set of plants. Remember, it is important to steer clear of seeds belonging to weaker plants, as they will end up being dead weight. If you are buying your seeds from a gardener then ask him to give you a blend of good seeds. The same rule extends to cuttings. Ensure that you pick plants that carry good genes.

Dark jars

Making use of dark colored glasses to store the buds will ensure your cannabis matures faster. Light can delay the process of curing and thus, darker jars will provide for the ideal medium to cure your buds. Placing the jars in a dark place will further enhance their maturity.

Light

Although buds like it dark when it comes to curing, the plant loves light during the growing stages. Providing it with enough natural or artificial light ensures that the plants grow stronger and faster. Remember, the more the light, more the number of buds you will remain with during harvest. Bright light also ensures that the buds and leaves reach their full potential and leave behind a strong THC content.

Supplements and enhancers

Apart from the nutrients feed to your cannabis plants, sufficient supplements and enhancers must also be provided. These supplements will give the plant a much-needed boost and enhance their chemical content. Bloom enhancers and shooting powders are your best bet. Bloom enhancers such as humic acid and trace minerals will not only enhance the quality of the existing buds but also increase their number. Shooting powders contain phosphorus and potassium. Phosphorous enhances the number of flowers and potassium increases their weight. Adding them once every two weeks will leave you with a great yield.

Coco coir

Coco coir is a soil additive that goes a long way in enhancing both the quality and yield of cannabis plants. Coco coir is a natural substance derived from the husk of coconuts. It is rich in many vitamins and nutrients capable of enhancing plant health. What's more, the coir helps the roots of the plant absorb the nutrients better. It also has a better water holding capacity thereby reducing the need to water your plants regularly. Add about 5 tablespoons of coco coir to the plants every 3 to 4 weeks. It also makes for a great growing medium. Start your cannabis plants in coco coir before transplanting them to end up with healthy saplings.

Temperature and humidity

Temperature can make or break your cannabis plants. You have to be careful with the maintenance of both day and nighttime temperature levels. Morning temperatures should remain between 65 and 80 degrees Fahrenheit, while nighttime levels should remain within 80 and 90 degrees Fahrenheit. This will make sure plants grow faster and healthier. Cannabis plants require maximum humidity during the growth stage and minimal humidity during flowering and harvesting stage. Make use of a scale to measure the humidity from time to time and move the plants around the room to ensure their comfort.

Cleanliness

It pays to keep your garden as clean and spotless as possible while growing cannabis. Right from the tools to the surroundings and your hands, keep everything clean to remain with a good yield. While pruning and drying plants, ensure that you wear good quality gloves. Also make sure the jars used to cure and store the weed are thoroughly cleansed and sterilized in advance. The drying room should be free of dust and dirt and have plenty of fresh air circulating.

Natural Pesticides

Chemical pesticides can potentially damage cannabis plants. But not using pesticides can result in the development of an insect menace. The best way to deal with this issue is to make use of a natural pesticide. Mix 1-tablespoon neem oil to a bottle of water along with a quarter teaspoon of soap powder. Shake it thoroughly and spray on the plant from a good distance. Make sure you do not exceed this limit as it can potentially damage your plants. Use this every 3 weeks to keep pests at bay. Also consider adding good quality neem powder to the soil to effectively deal with pests.

Decarboxylating cannabis

Decarboxylating is a very important step of the process. You have to first activate the chemicals within the leaves, flowers and buds to avail its full benefits. Here are the steps to follow in order to decarboxylate your cannabis.

- Preheat the oven to 240 degrees Fahrenheit.
- Cut up the leaves, buds and flowers into bite sized pieces. Be careful so as to not cut them too small as that can result in their burning.
- Place a baking sheet over the tray and place all the leaves, flowers and buds over it. Cover every inch of the paper and leave no gaps.
- Stick the tray into the oven for 30 to 40 minutes or until the leaves, buds and flowers crisp up.
- Check a few pieces to see if they crumble between your fingers.
- Use your palms to rub the leaves, flowers and buds and separate the seeds from it.
- Save the seeds for future use.
- Add the crushed cannabis to a glass jar for proper storage.

Canna oil recipe

Canna oil is what is mostly used to prepare foods. A little can go a long way in providing you with a healthy mind and body. The oil can also be used superficially to avail relief from aches and pains. Here is a simple recipe to follow.

Ingredients:
- 1 cup decarboxylated canna leaves
- 2 cups vegetable or olive oil
- Large strainer

Recipe:
1. Add the decarboxylated and crushed leaves to a bowl.
2. Add in the vegetable oil and mix until well combined.
3. Add the mix to a boil and place on low heat.
4. Cook it for 6 to 8 hours, stirring occasionally.
5. You can also use a crockpot for this process and keep it on low for 8 hours.
6. Once done, strain the oil through the large strainer and collect it in a jar.
7. Place the jar in a dark place to let it mature.
8. Use instead of regular cooking oil.

Cannabutter recipe

Cannabutter is a good replacement for canna oil. It can be used to prepare dishes and also makes for a good external applicator to ease joint pains. Here is a simple recipe to follow.

Ingredients:
- 1 cup decarboxylated canna leaves
- 1 cup plain unsalted butter

Recipe:
1. Make use of room temperature butter to beat and soften.
2. Preheat the oven to 240 degrees Fahrenheit.
3. Add in chopped decarboxylated leaves to it and mix until well combined.
4. Place it in the oven for 5 minutes.
5. Once done, mix it well and allow cooling down.
6. Stick it in the fridge/freezer to harden completely.

NOTE: It is safe to feed both canna-oil and cannabutter to children but in controlled quantities.

Chapter 7: Cannabis Medical Uses

Cannabis plants are used to serve several medicinal purposes. Here is looking at some of the important ones.

Glaucoma

Cannabis helps in treating glaucoma. The condition is a result of pressure that builds up inside the eye. Smoking marijuana on a regular basis can combat this. As per studies, smoking the drug lowers the pressure inside the eye and relieves the pain. It will pay to smoke good quality cannabis to avail its full medical benefits.

Epilepsy

Epilepsy is a condition that occurs due to a sudden change in brain signals. Although there is no sure cure for the condition, it is possible to treat it to a certain extent. As per studies, those that smoked cannabis on a regular basis were able to control their epilepsy to a large extent. Seizures occurred less often and the person was able to maintain good mental health.

Cancer

CBD present in cannabis is said to bind with cancerous cells and stop its growth in the body. Research conducted on breast cancer cells revealed that it is beneficial to consume any form of cannabis as it can, to a certain extent, stop the growth and production of cancerous cells.

Anxiety

Regular consumption of cannabis is said to aid in the reduction of anxiety and depression. THC helps in duplicating dopamine in the brain, which automatically encourages the release of serotonin. This helps in enhancing the mood and controlling anxiety to a large extent. This effect will only grow over time and increase your mental capacity.

Alzheimer's disease

Smoking cannabis regularly can greatly help with combating Alzheimer's disease. It is an old age illness that affects brain health. As per studies, those who were exposed to cannabis pills were in a better position to combat the onset of the illness. THC assists in blocking the amyloid plaques in the brain thereby reducing the onset of Alzheimer's.

Spasms

Cannabis can help in reducing muscle spasms. This is a problem most relevant to athletes. Consuming cannabis products, such as pills and syrups, can successfully cure minor aches and pulls. It is a great way to deal with sports injuries and also prevent their occurrences to a large extent.

Arthritis

Arthritis is a painful condition that results in the swelling of joints. CBN present in cannabis helps in reducing the inflammation between the joints and encourages easy movement. It also facilitates lubrication between joints thereby reducing the pain associated with the condition. Consuming pills containing THC on a regular basis can help reduce the side effects of arthritis.

Nausea

Cannabis can help in combating nausea. Patients suffering from nausea and sickness after chemotherapy experienced a great relief after consuming pills containing cannabidiol.

ADHD

Studies have shown a relation between consuming cannabis pills and controlling the effects of ADHD. It is apparent in both adults and children and is now being considered as a safe solution to consider.

Weight loss

It is pretty easy to cut down on excess weight by consuming pills containing THC and CBN. Both assist in lowering appetite levels and cut down on fat cells in the body. Those looking to maintain their figure can also turn to cannabis to help them with their cause.

Cutting down drinking

Cannabis is said to help with cutting down on drinking habits. If you suffer from such a habit then can turn to cannabis smoking to help you with the cause.

These are just some of the many benefits that cannabis can provide. If for some reason you have consumed or inhaled too much of the herb, then here are a few quick solutions to reduce its effect on your mind and body.

- Drink plenty of water. This will flush out a majority of the chemical from your body
- Drink a mixture of orange and lemon juice
- Inhale a strong scent
- Eat fresh fruits

If you still feel high then sleep it off!

Conclusion

The main aim of this book was to educate you on the basics of growing cannabis plants and how to use it in cooking. Once you get going, you will know how easy it is to both grow and maintain your weed plants. Feel free to switch it up between growing them indoors and outdoors and maintain a constant supply.

We also looked at how to harvest and store it to ensure that you have a good quantity available with you. I have done my bit by teaching you about the growing process. It is now entirely up to you to put the steps to practice and start growing your own weed!

I wish you luck with your endeavors and hope you have a great time harvesting your plants!

Hydroponics and Aquaponics for Beginners

The Complete Guide on How to Build a Hydroponic Garden & Aquaponic System

Monica Jacobs

Table of Contents

Introduction

Gardening can be a really peaceful activity when done right. It's the favorite hobby of a lot of people because there's something exhilarating about growing something with your own hands and seeing it develop and grow. It's always fun to take pick the fresh produce out of the garden to consume it.

Traditional gardening can be extremely tiring because you have to fight against the seasonal bugs, lack of nutritious soil and the perpetual weeds. Many people give up on traditional gardening because it's simply not worth the effort.

Hydroponic gardening is a revolutionary way to grow plants by focusing on water instead of soil. All you have to do is add in a little bit of nutrient solution to the water and use a pump to move the water around. So, you will be able to grow plants in a better way without fighting against issues that are present in traditional gardening.

Anybody can follow this process and garden without even putting in too much effort. This book is a simple guide that will teach you all about Hydroponics so that you can start your very own garden by following the simple steps shown in this book. It's easy and fun as well as very satisfying.

Thanks again for downloading this book, I hope you enjoy it!

Chapter 1: Basics of Hydroponics

Before you can get too far into this process, you first need to understand what hydroponics is even about. First off, it is a type of gardening. While most people will start out with a nice plant in the yard or by using pots to make their plants grow, with a lot of soil and other things that will help make it easier, hydroponics is going to tackle this in a different manner. It recognizes that things don't always work as well with the traditional methods and that soil isn't necessary to help your plants grow big and strong.

So, hydroponics is basically a process where water is distributed, making sure to preserve the quality, and still providing the nutrients that the plants need to reach their full potential. This basically includes adding in some nutrients that the plants will need to the water that you provide them with, so the soil is not important. When you plant your produce in your garden, you are relying on the rain to help out with the process. The dirt is going to have a lot of the nutrients that your plants need in order to be strong and healthy. But the plants are not able to get all this goodness out on their own. Rather, the process waits for the rain to come, which then releases the nutrients and gives these to the plants. But when rain doesn't come, or you don't water your plants, you are not only dehydrating the plants, but you are keeping the nutrients in the soil away from the plants.

While this may seem like an easy process for the plants to get their nutrients, it is not perfect. There are times when there isn't enough rain. The soil may not have enough of the nutrients in it at all due to regional conditions and the plants can't thrive because of this lack of nutrients. Or perhaps the nutrients are too far down in the soil for the water to be of sufficient help. No matter what the reason, this can make it really hard to provide the plant with the nutrients that it needs.

Since the natural way of providing nutrients to the plants is not always as effective as we may hope, hydroponics is sometimes used to overcome this anomaly. The goal of this process is to do a replication of the natural setting, but it is designed to make this work better. The way that this is done is by adding nutrients into the water and helping it to enrich the plants in the process. When the right nutrients are in the water, the plants are able to absorb them and grow healthier and stronger. If you do this process right, the plants will be able to grow better than they would in your own garden or another spot outside.

The nutrient solution is often up to you to create. You will usually need to make an enclosed system in order to move those nutrients around to the right place. The enclosed options used in hydroponics are great because they can also avoid the issue of evaporation so the plants can get all of the nutrients without the water evaporating. The water will always be there and you don't have to worry about the nutrients getting lost in the soil or that the water will disappear before all of the nutrients are absorbed. This method is super efficient and puts you in control of feeding your plants the goodness they need.

There are a few different ways that you can set up your hydroponics. These are man-made so there are different choices and you will need to pick the one that is right for your garden, such as taking into account the size of growing area that you want and the right kinds of plants to suit your needs. You may want to look up a few plans to see what is available and which ones you will be able to get into the space you have available. Planning is everything.

Benefits of Hydroponics

Farming and gardening techniques are changing and improving, much like technology. The soil-less technique or hydroponics is fast becoming popular because it gives farmers and gardeners less to worry about.

Hydroponics allows plants to grow in nutrient solutions instead of soil that leaves tilling, weeding, fertilizing, pesticide spraying and cultivation out of the picture. Moreover, bigger crop results can be achieved in shorter amounts of time. It is an easy and more efficient way to grow vegetables, fruits and flowers. In addition, the produce is healthier and contains more nutrient value.

Hydroponic gardens can be maintained indoors and outdoors and are very undemanding and inexpensive to maintain.

Here are some key advantages to using hydroponic systems:

- Hydroponic gardens require no soil. So even if you live in an area where soil quality is poor, your plants will thrive. Crops can be grown in greenhouses and even in desert regions.

- Hydroponic gardens require less land surface. Plants can be grown in mediums that can be placed in high-density areas or multi-story buildings. The hydro units can also be stacked.

- ·Hydroponic gardening ensures a high yield in a controlled environment. The needed nutrient environment can be maintained and provided to ensure plant growth and productivity. Compared to soil cultures, a small space can produce up to about ten times the size of plant matter.

- Hydroponics promotes water conservation. Plants are given the accurate amount of water that they need. If you grow plants in soil, you will require 90% more water to nourish the plant compared to a properly designed hydroponics system. Labor for watering is also avoided as the water stays in the hydroponic system.

- Hydroponic gardens and farms can be set up in places with cheap water and power. When established in close proximity to places where there is a high demand for a particular crop, transport and shipping costs are reduced.

- Hydroponic gardening eliminates the need for pesticide and herbicide. It is possible to go organic with this set-up. Likewise, it is easier to eliminate plant diseases and pests.

- Hydroponic gardening ensures that there is no nutrition pollution to the environment. Aeration is made possible and the risk of calcium, potassium, and phosphorus run-off is easily prevented.

- Hydroponic gardeners and farmers do not have to mulch, weed, till and change the soil. They also don't need to add fertilizer to soil and it is also easy to harvest crops.

Disadvantages of Hydroponics

There are many benefits to hydroponic gardening. Lack of land, a frequent supply of water and other environmental concerns can be conquered with hydroponics. With the right knowledge and proper techniques, it is a valuable system for commercial farmers and gardeners. But while hydroponics poses a lot of benefits to modern gardening and farming, there are also disadvantages that need to be considered.

For one, the initial cost to set-up a properly designed and effective hydroponic system is high. In the long run, the conservation of water and nutrients may prove to be inexpensive but before you can enjoy those benefits, you need to set-up a hydroponic system with all the necessary equipment. Hydroponic equipment does not come cheap. Additionally, technical knowledge and skills are required to maintain the equipment.

Other disadvantages of hydroponic garden systems are the following:

- Compared to farming in large fields, hydroponic gardening may yield a limited production.

- Hydroponic gardening requires constant supervision. You need to be responsible and diligent because the plants depend on you for their survival.

- If you do not have sufficient knowledge, you be depending on trial and error. Some plants will flourish while others may die. You should be prepared to encounter frustrations and disappointments.

- Hydroponic gardens are interrupted and influenced by power outages and pump failures.

- Because there is no soil to act as a buffer, the plant will wither and die rapidly once the system fails. If interruptions occur, the plants must be watered manually.

- Should a water-borne organism or disease appear in your set-up, it will quickly spread and all plants will be easily affected. Hence, vegetative growth and production are disturbed.

As with any project, make sure you consider all aspects and count the costs before you decide to set-up your own hydroponic system.

Chapter 2: History of Hydroponics

The system and technique of Hydroponics are not new. People have been using hydroponics and other related forms of hydro cultivation since ancient times. To understand the modern hydroponics as well as to have a thorough knowledge of the system, it is necessary to study the history of Hydroponics briefly. In this chapter, I have tried to put down all the relevant history that can be used to prove the importance, as well as the historic and ancient nature, of the system of hydroponic gardening.

Instead of going by the regular timeline - from the beginning of the ancient era to the recent times - I will start with the recent years and will stop at the ancient era simply because a lot of information is available about recent developments related to hydroponic gardening as compared to the ancient era.

The earliest written documents talking about cultivation without soil was a book called Sylva Sylvarum that was published in the year 1627. The world famous polymath, Francis Bacon, wrote it. Printed a year after his death, Bacon's book deals with simple cultivation techniques for cultivating terrestrial plants without soil. Within just a few decades, cultivation without soil or water culture became a research phenomenon in 1699. People all over the Europe started experimenting with water culture and cultivation and documented this work extensively. One such person was John Woodward who wrote detailed documents on his experiment of growing spearmint with water culture. According to his research, he postulated that plants thrive and grow better in impure or rather normal water sources as compared to distilled or 'clean' water. But people back then did not know what exactly enabled and helped the plants to grow. They knew about the fertilizers etc. but the elements and chemicals that assisted the process were still unknown.

Research regarding these elements etc. was extensive and finally, after 100+ years, scientists were successful in identifying them. By the year 1842, a small list of nine elements essential for the thriving of plants was made. The German botanists, Wilhelm Knopf and Julius von Sachs, discovered the many intricacies of water culture and cultivation without the use of soil. With extensive research of around 6 years, from 1859 to 1865, these two botanists perfected the technique of this kind of cultivation. This was the era when solution culture came into existence.

Solution culture means growing and cultivating terrestrial plants without the use of soil. Instead of soil, solutions of mineral nutrients are used. This technique became immensely popular in that era and still enjoys a considerable amount of popularity. It is still used in teaching etc. Solutions are now supposed to be a part of hydroponics without the use of the inert medium.

In the last century, the research related to hydroponics and related systems achieved interest like never before. Solution culture was still very popular and in 1929, William Fredrick Guericke, of the University of California (Berkley), promoted solution culture publicly to increase the efficiency of agriculture. Guericke was also one of the first people who called this system aquaculture but when he found that the term is already used for fish farming etc. he decided to change it.

Guericke created a huge uproar and established his name in history by growing tomato vines measuring 25 feet in height in his backyard with the help of nutrient solutions instead of soil.

Around the year 1937, this proficient scientist invented or rather introduced the term hydroponics. He introduced the term with the help of W.A. Setchell who was a famous classicist and psychologist. Guericke's successful experiments and claims

HYDROPONICS AND AQUAPONICS FOR BEGINNERS

that hydroponics would revolutionize cultivation and agriculture attracted widespread attention. He received numerous letters asking for more information on his research.

In 1940, Guericke published his guide called 'Complete Guide to Soilless Gardening.' After this, many other types of research began slowly, and one day in Wake Island in the Pacific Ocean, hydroponics was used to grow vegetables for the consumption of passengers in the year 1930. It solved the expensive problem of airlifting vegetables to the island. As the soil was not available on the island, hydroponics proved to be a blessing for the airlines.

In the 1960s, Allen Cooper, a scientist from England, devised a new technique called the Nutrient Film technique. In 1982, at WorldFu's EPCOT center, the Land Pavilion prominently featured various uses of hydroponic gardening and cultivation. In recent times, even NASA has been doing extensive work and research on Hydroponics.

Tracing the history of hydroponics, we can easily go back to the time of Babylon. Although most of these historical sites claim to have been based on hydroponics, it cannot be proven whether they were really based on the hydroponic principles or some other forms of aquatic cultivation. Nevertheless, they hold a distinct place in the history of hydroponics because they prove that cultivation without soil is not a new phenomenon.

Hanging Gardens of Babylon

The Hanging Gardens of Babylon are considered as one of the most beautiful wonders of the ancient world. This extensive complex was supposed to have ornamental and flowering plants from not only Asia but also the whole world. These plants were supposed to hang from pillars and arches etc. in a decorative fashion.

As Babylon was situated in a very hot and arid region, growing all of these plants in such area was considered impossible. It is thus believed that all of these plants were grown and irrigated with the help of the water from the river Euphrates.

The history of the gardens is rather mythical because it is not clear whether Nebuchadnezzar ordered it or Sammu-ramat. Even the era of construction is not clear as some historians claim it to be between the 8th – 7th century BC,

The construction was believed to be done on the top of ziggurats and the plants got their water from channels. Although these gardens are quite famous, the evidence of the existence of such a massive structure is missing. It is nowadays considered to be a matter of controversy and no solid proofs are available.

According to Robert Koldewey, there is archaeological evidence that proves that the technology used for the gardens was scientifically valid and thus the gardens could have existed. Ancient Greek men such as Siculus, Diodorus and Strabo have written notes on Hanging Gardens.

Whether or not these gardens existed, the technology did and that matters.

Chinampa

Although the existence of the Hanging Garden is controversial, the existence of Chinampa is well documented. Chinampa is a floating armada situated on a lake in Xocimilco region, situated in Chinampan, Mexico. The garden was in existence in the era of the Aztecs and it is believed that this garden had an undeniable role in the flourishing of the Aztecs.

A considerable amount of the garden is still in use today.

Chapter 3: Creating your Hydroponic Garden

So now that you have a good idea of what a hydroponic garden is all about, it is time to actually create your own garden. Don't worry, this is not a complicated process and it works well even for beginners, but it is still going to take some time to get it under control. Making the right hydroponic medium is the next step to help you get started with this process.

Choosing the right Medium

The hydroponic medium is going to be really helpful throughout the process; without this medium, you will find that the plants are not able to grow in the way that you would like. There are a few things that the perfect medium needs to have in order to work well for your garden. The first thing is that the medium should have the capacity to hold equal amounts of air and water inside.

While most people don't spend much time thinking about oxygen when it comes to plants, your plant will not be able to survive without any oxygen or just on water. Oxygen is important for allowing some respiration to the plant so it can absorb the nutrients and water that you provide and it can use this to grow bigger.

To find a medium that is going to be able to balance the water and the air, you need to find one that has the right amount of holes in each fragment, or the interstitial spaces.

When picking out your medium, you need to make sure that it is affordable as well. There are many varieties of these hydroponic mediums that you can choose from but having one that isn't too expensive should be the goal. You want to find something that can Soilless as well. It doesn't make much sense to spend money on this system and then throw it away at the end of the season.

There are some great options that you can choose when it comes to your hydroponic medium. Some of the options that you can choose include:

Gravel

One of the most commonly used, and simple to find, substrate is gravel. Gravel can frequently be found in the ebb and flow system because of its weight and durability. With that benefit, however, is also what makes it problematic. Gravel can be difficult to carry around because it's heavy and can damage plants if you're not careful.

Another pitfall is that gravel is not porous at all and retains no water. You can't count on it if you have a power outage so be sure if you do choose gravel that you watch the water nutrient levels and be sure that your plants are not drying out.

Perlite

Perlite is a unique medium but can be a lot of fun to use in your gardening. It is a volcanic glass that is really good at holding onto oxygen for the plant to use. It works really well for this kind of garden, but you do need to remember that this material is lightweight. If you live in an area that is windy and things can be knocked down quickly, you will need to pick out another material so the garden isn't ruined.

Starter Sponges

Starter sponges are one of the best options when it comes to starting out your hydroponic garden as a beginner. These are perfect for protecting the root and adding in the perfect amount of water and air to the plant. There are many different sizes so it is important to choose whether your garden is going to be big or small, as they are easy to start mediums. Most beginners will start with this option because it is easy to use and you will be able to find them all over the place when you're ready to start.

Leca

This stands for Lightweight Expanded Clay Aggregate and it is a good medium to go with if you want something that is natural. It comes from clay granules that have been expanded. The pH levels are neutral so you won't have to worry about this causing some damage to the plants and it is able to retain water at high levels so it is good as a rooting solution.

Rockwood

This is a derivative of melted rock that has been made into fibers; this medium is good if you would like to do hydroponics on a large scale. This choice is going to be good for retaining water so the plants get all of their nutrients and sufficient hydration. It is also good at keeping all the contaminants out of the hydroponic system so the plants won't get a disease or anything else that will harm them. It is a good medium to use, but if you are worried about the environment, the materials in this choice are not made in the most environmentally friendly way.

Coconut Fiber

This is an organic material that is great for this kind of growing. It is able to hold air and water perfectly and has the added bonus of being able to protect the plants from fungus. There are several different names that this comes under so you should look around for it. You will find it as a compressed block that will expand as soon as you place it into some water.

It is reusable so you can keep it for several years and keep your hydroponic garden growing.

As you can see, there are quite a few different options that you can pick from when it comes to choosing your medium. You may want to check all of them out and see which one is going to work the best for you. Some are better for bigger gardens while others are best for the smaller gardens. Some are good with fungus prevention, which can be important in some parts of the country. Mix and match a bit and you will find that it is easier than ever to find the right medium for your garden. Also talk to suppliers as they will have experience in your area.

Choosing a Hydroponic System

The next thing that you need to figure out is the hydroponic system. This is the system that helps you to create the perfect conditions for your plants. It will help the roots to get the perfect amounts of oxygen, water and nutrients that your plants need. With the passive system, you will rely on gravity to help keep the plants happy.

There are several different options that you can choose with each of these systems and often it will depend on what works the best for you. Some people like the idea of gravity because they don't have to do as much work, but you will have to worry about moving the nutrients around. The active option works nicely because you can let it go for some time, such as when you leave to go on a trip, and the plants will still be taken care of. Let's look at a few of the most popular options that you can choose from in order to get the very best out of your hydroponic system.

Wick System

The first set up is called the Wick System. This system is by far the easiest of the six and has the simplest of designs for someone starting out. The design is made up of a passive type system with no moving parts. Since the wick system uses this passive set up, it makes it not only cheaper to start, but it's also easy to maintain.

The positives to these types of systems are many, but there are a few drawbacks as well. Plants that require a lot of water, or thirsty plants, such as tomatoes do not do well in these types of systems. When you are using a wick system the ideal plants to grow are typically quick growing plants, such as herbs and lettuces. This is important to keep in mind when choosing a system based on what you plan to use it for. The key factor of a wick system is that it uses more than one wick that will deliver the water to the roots of the plants, from the reservoir. The setup of a wick system typically is made up of four components; grow tray, wick, aeration and reservoir.

In order for you to really understand, it's important that we define the terminology that will show up from time to time. A wick, by definition, is a cord or thread of roughly woven, or twisted braids - something similar to a cotton rope, and this soaks up the liquid. So now that we know what the wick is, what exactly is the capillary action? This is the interaction between the liquid, in this case the nutrient-rich water, and the solid, the rope. The two meet and the liquid travels through the rope. This is how the liquid reaches the plant through the wick. The growth tray with a wick system differs from all other setups in that it uses a growing medium to entirely fill up a tray, and does not use net pots. The growth trays can be anything that you use which is moveable and contain the mess of your plants, such as the substrate or medium. The kind of medium used should be one that drains slowly, allowing the full use of the capillary action. Each medium plays a key element in the support of your setup. Some of the most common mediums used are Perlite and Vermiculite. The reservoir with a wick system is basically the same as it is in any other hydroponic system. The reservoir is a large container containing fertilized water, which sits beneath the growth tray and feeds nutrient rich water to the plants.

The Nutrient Film Technique

So the first one we will look at is the NFT. Inside of this system, you will find a tunnel. The plants will be placed on this tunnel while the roots are inside of it. You can then place your nutrient solution into the tunnel and while the nutrient solution travels through the system, it is going to make some contact with the roots of the plants.

When the nutrient solution gets through the system, it is not going to just go to waste. Instead, this is going to work like a Dutch Bucket System. There is a pump on this system that will recycle your nutrient solution so it goes right back through your system again. It will keep going around in a loop until you take it out in order to add some new nutrients.

The biggest advantage that comes with this system is how it is completely enclosed. This helps to create a good level of humidity which the plants need to thrive. In addition, it is going to reduce any risk that you have of the roots becoming too dehydrated. This is also a good system to use for lettuce as well as other crops that are short-term.

Water Culture System

With a water culture system, things are different. The water culture system works entirely on filling up a reservoir and allowing the roots of your plants to bathe in the nutrient-rich solution, simultaneously using an air pump to flow oxygen to the plants as well. There is an ease of use with this type of system much like the wick system. There is only one piece of equipment to worry about, but you must pay close attention to your plants to avoid disaster. If there should be an issue with the air pump line, the plants can literally drown.

The key to making this system work is to make sure your air pump is always working. It may be beneficial to invest in a more expensive, better quality air pump if you can so that you can be rest assured your pump will always be performing at its best. Unlike the wick system, the water culture system uses netted pots. A netted pot is usually a small black pot with holes that allow for the free flow of water. As your plants grow, the nutrients in the water may need to be changed regularly as well.

Raft System

This is a good system for the beginner to choose because it is affordable and efficient. The plants will be put onto polystyrene sheets and then they float over the nutrient solution that you make. The roots of the plants will be exposed so they are getting the nutrients and the water that they need. The solution that is inside of the area will be circulated so that oxygenation occurs. This is another good system to choose if you have a plant that goes through some rapid growth cycles.

Dutch Bucket System

Beginners can use this option but commercial growers often save it for using with specific crops. It is really effective with some of the mediums that we discussed in the previous chapter so you get a lot of freedom with this one. If you are planting a crop that takes longer to grow, such as roses, basil, peppers, and tomatoes, this is the system to choose because it does well with these kinds of plants.

This system will need a PVC pipe to use as your drain tube and a large bucket. You will take your premade nutrient solution and place it into your bucket with the help of a dropper. This solution is then drained out with your drainpipe into a prepared reservoir, thanks to the use of gravity. You will then need to set up a pump that will take the nutrient solution and push it back into the bucket so this cycle is able to complete itself again.

This is a really efficient method to get your plants watered and happy, but you do need to be careful and set it up right. This system is usually saved for commercial growers who have a lot of plants to take care of at once, but if you have a bit of experience or are ready to do the whole setup, it can be a great way to take care of your plants with hydroponics.

Flood and Drain System

The Ebb and Flow system is also known as the Flood and Drain system. Basically what this means is that there is a growth tray holding your pots filled with a substrate of some kind. This could be clay pellets, wool or some other medium.

There is a timer on the system that will begin regularly scheduled intervals, which will trigger the start of the pump and fill the reservoir. The reservoir will fill until it can reach the roots of the plants and then drains the water back down when it is finished. The regularly set timers keep the roots of the plants sporadically covered in nutrients and air.

Today Ebb and Flow systems are typically found in home gardens for the beginner, also much like the wick system. There are a few drawbacks that make the ebb and flow system less desirable than other systems. The most notable is the fact that the roots tend to grow together, which means more work for the owner. They can spend more time than they would like to remove and harvest damaged plants. When you have this problem, the quality and yield of plants in these conditions are usually poor if not addressed. It can manifest in brown and yellow spots on the leaves as well.

Autopot Self-watering System

Many of those who are interested in getting started with hydroponics are short on space and worry that they are not going to be able to complete this process. This can be a problem with some of the other systems listed in this chapter, but the Autopot is the perfect solution. While it may take some time to get the Autopot set up, you will find that they are a passive method to use and are really good for plants that are slow at growing. This is a newer development so many people are not used to hearing about it, but the system does not take up a lot of space and is easy to use.

The nice thing about this process is that it is able to feed the plant on its own. This is possible thanks to the SmartValve that can feed all of your plants on demand; it will only release the water and nutrient solution when the plants need it, such as when the medium is going dry. This is also a great replication of natural rainfall so you are getting the very best to the plants that you use.

Drip System

The Drip System is the most widely used hydroponic system. It is set-up with a timer, a submerged pump and a grow tray. The timer is set to turn the pump on to allow the nutrient solution to drip off directly onto the plants through a tiny drip line. There are two kinds of Drip Systems: Recovery and Non-Recovery. In a Recovery Drip, the surplus nutrient solution that flows down is collected in a reservoir and re-used. In a Non-Recovery Drip, the nutrient solution that runs off is not collected.

The Recovery Drip System is more efficient and less expensive. Apart from being able to re-use the excess nutrient solution, the system does not need precise control for the watering cycles. The timer needs to be more precise in a Non-Recovery Drip System so the plants get enough of the nutrient solution and there is minimal runoff.

The Recovery System requires more maintenance in recycling the solution back to the reservoir and the pH and strength of the nutrient solution needs to be preserved. This requires periodic testing and adjusting so that pH and strength levels do not shift. On the other hand, the Non-Recovery System needs less maintenance, as the solution is not re-used.

Aeroponics

Another system that you can use is the Aeroponic system. With this system, the plants are going to get water and nutrients to the roots while they are in mid-air. To use this system, you will need to take the plants and place them into baskets that are on the top of an enclosure. The roots are exposed in this enclosure and then you can spray them with the nutrient solution.

This is probably one of the most efficient methods to help take care of your plants. The roots are the only thing that you need to take care of and they just need the solution that you are using. Anything that they don't use is going to be recycled so you can reuse it later on. You will need to be careful about keeping the right amount of humidity around the plants so they stay hydrated as much as possible. Once you have this part done, you will find that the crops are going to grow so much faster compared to their counterparts that are grown using soil. In most cases, this process is best for those who are really limited on the amount of space they have, such as being in an apartment.

Picking the right system that is going to work for your plants is going to take some research as well as reliance on your personal preferences. Sometimes it has to do with the amount of space that you have in your home. Check out some of these options to see how easy it is to make your own hydroponic garden without all the hassle while making it still work for your own personal use.

Chapter 4: Managing Plant Nutrition

Now that you have the right medium set up as well as a good system that will help you to keep the plants healthy, it is time to move on to picking out the right nutrition that will work for your plants. 90 percent or more of each plant is going to be made up of a combination of nitrogen, oxygen, hydrogen and carbon. The plant will need to be able to find these elements in order to grow the way that you want it to.

Think of these elements in the same way as the nutrients that you need in your body. When you eat food, it is important to get the right amounts of carbs, protein, and fats to stay healthy. Your body will work to extract them from your food in order for you to grow properly. When it comes to plants, it is the same kind of idea. The plants will usually try and get these out of the soil, but when you are using the hydroponic system, you may have to work on the solution on your own.

Nutrients

To get started are the four main nutrients that all plants are going to need in order to grow well. These include:

Carbon—this takes up over 50 percent of the composition of your plant. Chlorophyll is the best way for your plant to get hold of this and the sugar that come from chlorophyll is important as well.

Hydrogen—this one is good for helping the roots absorb the nutrients that it needs. In most cases, you will see that the plant will get its hydrogen from the water you provide.

Oxygen—this helps the plant go through respiration so it can grow through the process of creating starches and sugars.

Nitrogen—the nitrogen is able to create chlorophyll and amino acids that help to manufacture the sugars it needs to grow.

Without these nutrients, the plant is going to have some issues with growing and producing the way that you would like. Make sure that when you create your own nutrient solution or purchase one, you are careful about getting the right amounts of these into the mixture for a happy and healthy plant.

While the macronutrients are the most important for your plant because the plant will not be able to grow at all and develop without them, it is also really important to get those micronutrients in place as well. The plant will need less of these compared to the other nutrients, but adding them into the mix will help your plant to flourish and look as amazing as you had hoped.

There are many micronutrients that you can choose for your plant, and each of the premade soils will come with different varieties. Some of the nutrients that you should consider include:

Calcium—this one is great for helping the plant create more cell walls. If there isn't enough of this in your plant, it could have a slowing down of growth.

Sulfur—this nutrient helps the plant to synthesize proteins.

Iron—this one is good for sugar creation as well as chlorophyll development.

Magnesium—this one helps with creating enzymes and chlorophyll that help keep the plant strong. If your plant doesn't get enough of this, the leaves could start to yellow.

Boron—this one works hand in hand with calcium to make more cell walls. Too little of boron in the plant diet could result in some weak stems.

Manganese—creates oxygen during the process of photosynthesis. This one can also cause yellow leaves if not properly taken into the plant.

Zinc—zinc is really important to the plant because it helps with nitrogen, chlorophyll and respiration metabolism. If your plant has smaller leaves, it is probably short on zinc.

Copper—this nutrient helps with photosynthesis, respiration, and enzyme activation. Yellow and pale leaves are common in plants that are short on this nutrient.

Making your own nutrient solution, or purchasing one that is already made, that has the right amount of these micronutrients can make all the difference in the kind of growth you get out of your plants each year. Take the time to check out your nutrient solution to ensure you are giving your plants the very best.

Nutrient Solution

If you are a beginner with hydroponics, you may choose to just purchase a nutrient solution. This saves you some time and since there are so many good ones to choose, it helps you to get through the process, at least for the first year, without having to worry about having the right nutrients or other issues.

When you look at the solution, you will notice that there are percentages for NP- K on the package. These are important nutrients and you should make sure that they make up the majority of the solution. The higher concentration they are, the better this solution is for your plants. The rest of the solution is often going to be filler, although the good brands will have other micronutrients that are good for your plants.

This is not an area to skimp on when it comes to your hydroponic garden. While you may be interested in saving some money along the way, this is the main source of nutrients that your plants will get. They will not find nutrients from the soil or other locations, so you are responsible for getting the right solution to help out. Look for the best one you can find that has a lot of healthy nutrients and your plants are going to grow better than ever before.

After going through this process a few times, you may feel that it is time to take on the challenge and create some of your own solutions in the process. This is a bit trickier, but it does ensure that you are giving your plants the very best when it comes to their nutrition. You can choose to do this as a beginner, but remember it is a bit trickier and you will have to find all the ingredients on your own. If you are interested in doing this process, here are some easy formulas that can make your crops grow like crazy.

Vegetable Crops

- 6 grams of Calcium Nitrate
- .46 grams of Sulfate of Potash
- 2.09 grams of Potassium Nitrate
- 1.39 grams of Monopotassium Phosphate
- .4 grams of 7 percent Fe Chelated Trace Elements
- 2.42 grams of Magnesium Sulfate

Fruit Crop

- 8 grams Calcium Nitrate
- 1.70 grams Sulfate of Potash
- 2.80 grams of Potassium Nitrate
- 1.30 grams of Monopotassium Phosphate
- .40 grams trace elements
- 2/4 grams of Magnesium Sulfate

Flowering Crops

- .46 grams Potassium Nitrate
- 4.10 grams Calcium Nitrate
- 1.39 grams Monopotassium Phosphate
- 1.39 grams Sulfate of Potash
- .40 grams trace elements
- 2.40 grams Magnesium Sulfate

When doing this process, consider dissolving each element one at a time. This ensures that the element is going to have the chance to dissolve completely for use. All of the formulas will need a gallon of water, so fill up a container with this amount, making the water warm, and then add each salt one at a time for the best results.

The trace elements are just as important as the rest, but you can usually get a mixture that has them all together. Make sure that you have some iron, manganese, zinc, copper, boron, and Molybdenum in the mixture to ensure that it is going to keep those plants looking nice and strong for a long time to come.

PH Importance

Another thing that you will have to watch out for when it comes to your plants is their PH level. If these numbers are too low, you could have some issues with the plants being able to flower the way that you want. On the other hand, if you have the pH too acidic, it is going to kill off the plant in the process. You may want to consider having a meter that will watch for the concentration of salts in the solution so that the pH stays pretty much the same. If the pH gets a little off, the plants are not going to grow as much as you would like.

For most plants, you will want to keep the pH around 6.0 to 6.5; going too much below or above this amount is going to make it bad for the plants. Find a good kit that you can use to check the pH on occasion to ensure that you are giving the plants the very best environment for them to grow in.

PH is the potential hydrogen-hydroxyl ion content. To make it easier, let's think about a scale where you are weighing two items. One side you have some acidic juice and on the other, you have some bread or your base. Much like the scale, when we use the pH in hydroponics it's important that the scale is weighed equally by both. Often overlooked, understanding and checking the pH level has a huge impact on the product you will grow.

Water has an equal balance of both hydrogen and hydroxyl and therefore has a neutral pH level of 7. Each level of pH in a solution multiplies as it increases. If the pH level in your solution is 4.0 then it contains ten times more acid than something where the pH level is 3.0 and so on. Based on your plants, what this means is if your pH level needs to be 6.0 to 7.0 you would have to adjust the pH level ten times more than the current level. I know it sounds complicated, but trust me, it's something that is good to know if you want to create a wonderful hydroponic system. Each type of plant will need a different pH level and it's nice to have a reference for it. Here are some of the common plant pH levels you may need to know in the future:

- CABBAGE 6.5-7.5
- CUCUMBERS 5.9-6.1
- LETTUCE 6.0-6.5
- PUMPKIN 5.1-6.6
- RADISH 6.0-7.0
- STRAWBERRIES 5.5-6.5
- TOMATOES 5.5-6.5

When you need to check or adjust your pH it is fairly simple and there are several ways to do so. Typically the best way to check your pH level is to purchase paper test strips, which have a dye and allow you to compare the color of your water with the levels they show you. The only issues with this are that often the color differences can be hard to distinguish between. Another way to check your pH levels would be to purchase a liquid pH test kit. With this test, you add a slight amount of dye to a water sample. Similar to using the test strips, this way is more accurate to read and often gives better results. Lastly, if you're a hardcore gardener, you can purchase a digital pH meter. Obviously the most accurate, they can come in big pieces of equipment or in something as small as a pen. Either way, you use an electrode to test the sample water and are given the results. Find the right supplies for what you're doing and be sure to have some on hand whenever you need to test the pH levels in your hydroponic garden.

So now you've checked the pH level but how do you adjust it? The easiest and most effective things to have on hand are phosphoric acid (to decrease your pH) and potassium hydroxide, (to increase your pH). These are relatively harmless things you can easily buy and keep on hand. If you're not comfortable using them you can buy pH adjusters at local stores where everything has been mixed and is ready to go. The only issues with these are that they often cause huge shifts in the pH level and are harder to control. Adjust the pH level in your system slowly and be sure to check it regularly, and more often, after a change has been made to be sure the pH level is doing what you want it to. Over time you will develop a system that works for you and will have no issues adjusting the pH level next time. Don't be alarmed if the pH levels go up over time this is normal just be sure to check it with some regularity.

Chapter 5: Practical Guide

So by this point, you have spent a lot of time working on getting your hydroponic garden set up and ready for the plants. That is a lot of work, but once you have the supplies, you will be able to reuse them in the future and save a lot of time.

This chapter is going to review some of the most important things that you need to remember before starting to grow as well as the best steps to help you give your new plants the best care that they can find in this kind of garden.

Important Tips

Before getting started on your garden, there are a few things that you need to keep in mind. These are critical if you would like to see some amazing results with your garden and not have all your work go to waste before you start. Some of the things that you should remember for this garden include:

- Keep a constant temperature — each plant will like a slightly different one, but work to keep it constant and at a level that keeps away bacteria.

- Fresh air—even if you are growing the plants inside, you should include some fresh air for best results.

- Provide some oxygen—this is important to the roots and you can do this through agitation or a pump.

- Keep up with the pH levels and keep it consistent.

- Keep the nutrient solution as consistent as possible to avoid issues.

Each plant is going to need some different help in order to grow the way that it should. Some plants need a lot of temperature and others like it when it is cold. You will need to take some time to research each plant type so you ensure you provide the right kind of care to your plants.

Focusing on Seeds

First, you will need to get the seeds started. These need to be done in a place that is away from the hydroponic system. Once the plants get larger, you will be able to move them over to the main system, but they need to be started in a separate area. The area that you start your seeds in should have high levels of humidity and the right medium. If you would like to speed up this process, consider using a seed-warming mat with your trays for the best results.

Closing the Plant

While starting from a seed is the option that most beginners are going to choose, there is another option. With this option, you will begin the process by taking a plant that already exists and then make a clone from it. You would take one of the growing tips and then replant so this new one can make its own roots. This will help it to grow up into an identical plant from the one it was taken from.

If you do decide to go for this kind of process, you will need to keep the same kinds of conditions compared to the seed process, but the nutrient solution only needs to be 25 percent for it.

Main System

It will take a bit of time to get the seeds or the cloned plant to grow enough to be moved. But once they are ready, you will be ready to go through and get it to look great and love the hydroponic system. You will be able to consider moving the plants as soon as the cuttings or the seeds are forming a root system that is noticeable. This process is the easiest when you are using starter sponges. This is because you can remove and then insert these plugs into the growing medium in your hydroponic system, and then you are done. But often you will use a different starting medium that is going to be looser. For these, use some basket liners to prevent things from getting messy or not working out the way that you would like.

Once you are able to transplant the plants with the roots that are still inside the medium, make sure to keep the light a bit lower than normal. You will need to do this for about 3 or 4 days so that the plants aren't taking on too much with the light and aren't going to be harmed in the process. Once you get past these first few days, you will be able to increase the light to the place that your plants need.

While this process does take a bit of patience and time to master, it is not hard. You will be able to get it down in no time and will love the way that your garden is able to grow and prosper in this great system.

Chapter 6: Safeguards

While hydroponic gardens are some of the best that you can make in terms of efficiency and how easy they are to use, there are some issues that you can come across in your first few years as you learn how to get the process down.

There are several risks that you will need to watch out for because they can hinder how well your plants are growing and flourishing. Luckily, hydroponics are easy to use and they will make it simple to avoid problems as long as you are aware and looking for them. Here are some of the issues that you can look for and try to prevent for the best hydroponic garden possible.

Algae and Fungi

If you have too much humidity near your plants, you could have issues with fungi growing. This is a delicate balance that you have to deal with. While having some humidity in place is critical for helping the plants to grow, once the levels get too high, the fungi are going to keep on growing and taking over the whole place. So make sure to watch out for the humidity levels and constantly check it.

In addition, you need to take some time to take care of your plants. Take away any dead leaves or stems from your garden so that the fungi don't have anything to feed around. You shouldn't overwater the plants or this could change the humidity levels as well.

Sometimes even your best efforts aren't going to work. Perhaps the heat and humidity outside are too high and the fungi are going to grow without you having any way to stop it. If the fungi come out during the growing system, be sure to use a high-quality fungicide that can kill it off without causing any harm to the plant. The earlier on you can catch the outbreak of fungi, the better chance you have of preventing any further issues. You can even use a cloth that is dry to help remove it if it happens to get onto a particular plant.

There is another fungus that is known to grow in the medium. You will notice that there is a thin layer on top of your growing medium. The best thing to do for this is add in a little bit more of the LECA medium onto the top of what is already there.. This is going to help soak up some of the extra moisture so you won't have to do much more to get it fixed.

Algae can take another toll on your plants and this is going to thrive when the plant receives a lot of light. It can occur in both the growing medium and the nutrient solution. The algae are going to compete with the plants to get all of the nutrient solution, making it hard for the plants to get what they need.
To prevent this issue, you should take care to prevent direct light rays from entering into the reservoir and make sure that the water never sits still or you could have some issues. If you do have some algae that come into the reservoir, you will need to stop the process and wash it out with some bleach. If the algae come along in the growing medium, you will need to wipe it all away.

Water Microbes

The next obstacle you are going to need to watch out for is water microbes. These can make your nutrient solution ineffective because they are going to mess with the solution. There are many microbes that can show up in the water and will make it lose its goodness and not work as efficiently. You will be able to tell when these harmful microbes are present in the brown roots and bad smells that occur since they are going to ruin the root systems of your plants. Usually, this occurs when the water is still and warm so you need to create the right environment that will prevent this bad stuff from happening.

The best thing that you can do to prevent these bad microbes is to keep the right temperature in the water so they can't grow. 68 to 75 degrees is a great temperature and try to not let it vary very much. A pump is a good thing to use because this keeps the water from being still and moves it all around. When the water stays still, it is going to encourage the microbes, but when it is moving, the oxygen promoted should be sufficient to deter bad microbes.

Keeping your solution in order is important and ensuring that no harmful bacteria are able to grow in the water and ruin all your hard work, make sure that you are following some of the tips above.

Pests and Diseases

Plants can suffer from a variety of diseases and can suffer an attack from pests. The elements that cause diseases in human beings and animals cause diseases, albeit of different kinds, to plants as well. These diseases can wreak havoc on your plants and your produce. Because of this, many people use all sorts of pesticides, insecticides etc. to protect their plants.

Hydroponic Gardening systems, especially the indoor gardening systems, are not that susceptible to diseases and pests because they do not come in contact with harmful elements that may cause them. There is a low chance of these elements entering your system.

The soil is considered one of the main culprits for transporting the bacteria and viruses that cause disease in plants. As hydroponic gardening is done without soil, it reduces the risk of contamination. Having said this, plants are more likely to contract disease from other plants. Plant diseases are carried from a host plant in favorable conditions.

Plants that grow outdoors in soil are also more susceptible to diseases because often they become weak due to the fluctuating environmental conditions such as too much shade, too much sun, too less water etc. Even nutrient deficiency, excessive nutrients or pH imbalance can induce disease as well. As you must have noticed, many of the above circumstances simply cannot happen in the indoor hydroponic system. Yet your plants can catch diseases through incorrect care.

There are many factors such as incorrect handling etc. that may cause your plants to suffer. One of the foremost reasons why your plants contract disease is because they are handled without being aware of hygiene. If you handle your plants and equipment without cleaning your hands, there is a high risk of contamination.

Most of these diseases need harsh chemical treatments that are not good for your plant's health in the long term. These chemicals can possess your hydroponic system and can singlehandedly destroy your harvest. Therefore, what can you do when your precious system is under attack of diseases?

Common Solution:

Instead of directly using the commercially available and harsh chemical treatments, try using simple homemade solutions. More than often these solutions clear out the infection. A solution that is popular amongst gardeners is the All Purpose

Cure Solution. To make this solution you need to mix baking soda, lemon or lime juice and a drop or two of dish detergent with water. Put this solution in a bottle that has a spray nozzle and spray it generously over the affected portion of your plant. Most of the time, this solution works wonder although you have to spray it frequently. Be aware that sometimes this isn't enough. In such a case, you can try using other options such as cayenne pepper, salt etc. but be careful while using them. If nothing works, you will have to use the chemicals to save your plants.

Now let us have a look at some of the most common diseases and disorders that can affect your plants.

- Root Rot

Root rot is a kind of fungus that destroys the roots of the plants by 'rotting' them. This disease thus can kill your plants since they depend on their root system.
Treatment: You can use a mild fungicide to cure this one. Gently cut away the affected parts of the root and spray the fungicide lightly over the roots.

- Black Mold

Black mold darkens or blackens the leaf. A grayish or blackish growth is often seen on the leaves of the affected plant. This mold often results in leaf drop.

Treatment: Using a soft toothbrush, scrub off the mold gently. Clean the affected leaves with a damp cloth and with the All Purpose solution mentioned above. Once again, clean the leaves with a clean damp cloth.

- Powdery Mildew

Powdery Mildew is one of the most common diseases of plants and it is found almost in every corner of the world. This is a form of fungus and it results in whitish, grayish spots that are seen on the underside of the leaves. The leaves dry up fast and then drop off. It is commonly found in areas where the humidity is generally high.

Treatment: Although this disease is very common, fortunately, it is very easy to cure as well. Just take the All Purpose solution mentioned above and spray it all over the affected leaves. With this, if you find that your leaf is being affected with the fungus, cut the leaf off as soon as possible.

- Damping Off

Damping off is a very dangerous disease that normally only attacks plants that are planted in soil. With this disease, the fungus attacks small plants around the portion of the stem that is the nearest to the soil. The affected portion becomes weak or rots and the plant falls over and dies. This can also happen in hydroponic systems except that instead of soil the plants die in the water.

Treatment: Remove the diseased sections of the plants. If this is not possible simply, remove the plants from the system before the other plants contract the disease. Clean the container in which your affected plant was planted before planting anything new in it.

- Anthracnose

This happens in normal circumstances when the plant is overwatered. It causes dark marks on the leaves that fry them and finally these leaves drop off.

Treatment: Cut off the damaged or affected leaf and then spray the plant mildly with a fungicide.

- Rust

This highly contagious disease occurs mostly in highly humid areas. The symptoms of this disease include raised powdery pustules. These are scarlet red in color and are commonly seen on the undersides of the leaves. These can turn the leaves yellow and can make them drop off. The plant may die too.

Treatment: This cannot be treated with simple tools and you need to use harsh chemicals to treat it. Cut off the affected leaves if they are few in number and then use chemicals like maneb or zined.

- Crown and Stem Rot

This is a very common fungus that can cause the plant to get pulpy and rot away.
Treatment: Cut off the rotten and affected area as soon as possible. Spray the plant with a fungicide.

- Botrytis

This is commonly caused because of improper and inadequate ventilation. Grayish or whitish fuzz is seen on leaves. It is very uncommon in hydroponic gardens.

Treatment: Increase the ventilation and cut off the affected parts away.

- Early Blight

This is another very harmful disease that can kill a plant. Dark brownish black spots are seen on all the parts of the plant that can weaken it completely.

Treatment: This thing cannot be treated with simple tools and you need to use harsh chemicals to treat it. Cut off the affected parts if they are few in number and then use chemicals like maneb or zined.

- Club Root

This affects the growth of the plants. The roots of the affected plants turn into weirdly shaped tubers.

Treatment: Spray with a mild fungicide.

Conclusion

Hydroponic gardening has only now started to become mainstream but many people are still reluctant to try it. These people trust in traditional methods and believe that these new methods are too complex to handle.

But it's been scientifically proven that Hydroponics is a more efficient and beneficial way of gardening than traditional methods. So, if you follow the tips given in the book and set up the right system you'll be able to see how much more effective Hydroponics is than traditional gardening methods.

I hope that you were able to learn about Hydroponics from this book and understand the kind of benefits that you can glean when you use Hydroponic systems.

Cannabis Extract Guide

The Ultimate Guide On How to Make Marijuana Extracts For Cooking in Your Home, Including Cannabis Cookbook With 10 Recipes for Tasting Cannabis Cookies

Monica Jacobs

Introduction

I want to thank you and congratulate you for purchasing the book, "Cannabis Extract Guide".

This book contains proven steps and strategies on how to make Cannabis Extracts and Cannabis Cookies in your home like a pro.

While some of you may already be quite happily growing cannabis in your back garden or down in the cellar, there will be those who don't know where to start. I will give you a brief guide on how to grow your own cannabis, but for the most part, this book will concentrate on cannabis extraction methods and baking the most delicious cookies with your cannabis extracts.

Thanks again for purchasing this book, I hope you enjoy it!

Table of Contents

Chapter 1: A Brief Guide to Growing Cannabis

When it comes to growing your own cannabis, there are several steps that you need to follow for success. This is a brief guide to how to grow your own cannabis:

1. **Choose your location**

Are you growing indoors or outdoors? Indoor growing is a more private endeavor because it is away from prying eyes and it also gives you a higher level of control. It is also relatively cheap to set up an indoor cannabis farm, especially if you just want a couple of plants to keep you going. You can grow cannabis in a spare room, in your garage, in your basement, even in a closet.

One of the most important things about growing cannabis is to control your temperature although that isn't always possible if you choose to grow outside. Young cannabis plants need more warmth and will grow quicker when your temperatures are set to between 70 and 85° F – don't forget that, when your lighting is installed, that will raise the temperatures a little. When your plants are older, they will do better with cooler temperatures – between 65 and 80° F. This will help to produce the best buds.

Growing cannabis outdoors is even cheaper because the environment will do a lot of the work for you and you won't need to pay out for lighting or heating. However, you do need to keep an eye on things – if you live in a hot, dry climate, you will need to water your plants whereas, if your climate is rainy, you need to protect your plants from getting too much water.

2. **Lighting**

If you are growing indoors, there are several different types of lighting to choose from:

- CFL – compact fluorescent light bulbs
- LED grow lights
- Other fluorescent bulbs
- MH - Metal halide
- HPS - High-pressure sodium

Your plants need at least 8 hours of light per day so if growing outside they must be in direct sunlight for a minimum of 8 hours, preferably between 10 AM and 4 PM as this is when the sun is at its strongest and warmest.

If growing indoors, choose your lighting carefully. HPS and MH lights are the gold standard and provide the best overall lighting environment. They are powerful and cheap to buy and set up, as opposed to the LED lights, which are incredibly expensive. Many beginners start with CFL and move on to stronger lights for the flowering season

3. **Growing Medium**

Choose your growing medium carefully because each one has different requirements. The most common mediums are:

- Organic composted soil, full of nutrients
- soilless mixes – coco coir, vermiculite, perlite, etc.
- hydroponic – combined with MH or HPS lights, this provides the best and fastest growing medium

4. **Nutrients**

The type of nutrient required depends on the type of growing medium you are using. If you are using the composted soil, specifically made for cannabis plants, you will already have sufficient nutrients for the first stage of growing. From here on, and for those who are using hydroponic or soilless mediums, you will need to purchase specifically formulated cannabis nutrients. Alternatively, you can use something like Dyna-Grow at half strength. Dyna-grow is a two-system nutrient – one for the vegetative stage and one for the bloom stage.

As with all nutrient systems, don't start at full strength because you can burn your plants. You only need to raise the dose if your plants develop a problem like yellowing leaves or leaves dropping unless this occurs in the last couple of weeks before you harvest.

Always test the pH of your plants, which means testing your water before you introduce it. If you use composted super soil, you don't need to do this, as the microbial life in the soil will take care of the plants for you. Purchase a testing kit and stick to these general rules:

- For soil - 6.0 - 7.0
- For hydroponics – 5.5 – 6.5

5. **The plants**

If you know other growers, you can easily get your plants and know that they are a good strain. If you don't, you will need to purchase good quality seeds – you can do this online. You can also buy clone plants.

6. Seed Germination

If you have clone plants this section is irrelevant to you. For seed germination, the best way is to purchase a starter cube; keep it moist and warm and when the seedling appears you can put the entire cube into your chosen growing medium.

Another way is to place your seeds on paper towels on a plate, moisten it and cover with another plate. When the seedlings appear, you can transplant them.

7. Vegetation State

Once your plants have their first set of leaves they are classed as being in the vegetative stage. Keep the temperature constant and water regularly. Ensure that they have 18-24 hours of light per day if growing indoors and are in the strongest direct sunlight if growing outdoors.

8. Flowering

When your plants begin to bud, they are in the flowering stage. At this point, you will need to determine if your plants are male or female and discard the males. The males do not produce buds, only pollen sacs and are useless. You can ensure you get females by purchasing female clones or feminized seeds. You also need to change your lighting to 12 hours on and 12 hours off if growing indoors.

9. Harvesting

When your buds no longer produce new white hairs on them, you should be able to smell a strong cannabis smell. Wait for at least 40% of the hairs to turn a darker color and curl in – from here you can start harvesting. For the highest levels of THC (more about this later), harvest when between 50 and 70% of the hairs are dark.

10. **Drying and curing**

Hang your harvested buds' upside down in a dark and cool space with lots of ventilation so they can dry out. They should dry slowly and do make sure to check regularly for mold. Your buds are dry when the thin stems snap and the bigger stems are still a little bendy so now it's time to cure them to ensure a good smooth flavor.

Place the buds into mason jars, tightly closed and stored in a dark and cool place. Fill the jars ¾ full. Every day for the first 2 weeks, open the jars for a few seconds. This allows air in and moisture out. If your buds are moist, leave the lids off until they feel dry to the touch.

When the buds have been dry for at least 7 days, you can go down to removing the lid once a week. Cure for up to 30 days.

Chapter 2: A Brief History of Eating Cannabis

The very first drink with an onomatopoeic name was bhang because of the effect of your head feeling like it is exploding as you down it. Originating in India in the 10th century, bhang was the first product from experimentation with cannabis and its narcotic properties. By 1580, bhang was the most popular drink ever. But how was it made?

The leaves and the buds of the cannabis Sativa plant were ground using a mortar and pestle into a green paste and were then mixed with ghee, milk, and spices. Another recipe involved the boiling of the leaves first but the rest of the method was pretty much the same with the buds and leaves being mashed and mixed with sugar and water. These were then formed into small balls, names bhang goli, that were used as an aid to sleeping and consumed as an appetizer.

At around the same time, cannabis for cooking was also catching on in Europe. Bartolomeo, an Italian scholar from the 15th century published a book by the name of "On Honorable Pleasure and Health" and this contained a ganja recipe. Written in Latin, the recipe translates as:

"To make cannabis yourself more commonly used as flax for thread, use a mallet to crush clods [buds?] collected after a good harvest. Add cannabis to nard oil in an iron pot, crush together over some heat and liquefy into a health drink of cannabis nectar. Carefully treat food and divide for the

stomach and the head. Finally remember everything in excess may be harmful or criminal."

Even back then, in the 15th century, Platina was already beginning to talk like one of our modern-day potheads! And, if you can find a picture of him standing beside the Pope of the time when he was appointed to the Vatican, take a look at the eyes of both men – they look somewhat glazed!

Platina used heat as a way of rendering the THC but the Indians didn't do this so, is it possible that you can eat raw cannabis and still get high? The answer is yes, you can. It is an absolute myth that cannabis has to be cooked in oil or butter and that myth was totally debunked by a native of San Francisco, Alice B Toklas (1977 – 1967). Toklas was highly famous for her cooking and also for her cannabis baking, among friends such as Picasso, Hemingway, Matisse, and Paul Bowles. Bowles wrote, *"The user of cannabis is all too likely to see the truth where it exists and to fail to see it where it does not".*

We can only assume that Toklas gave her friends some of her well-known hash brownies, the recipe for which appeared in her 1954 book, The Alice B Toklas Cookbook. While this won't be seen as an issue by any pot heads, the problem with the recipe, called Hashish Fudge, was that it contained absolutely no hash whatsoever and neither did it have any chocolate in it. Toklas did not come up with the recipe herself; instead, it came to her via Brion Gysin, a performance artist, painter, and a friend of William S Burroughs. Also, there is no baking in this recipe – the ingredients are simply mashed together and rolled into balls, similar to the bhang goli from India. The recipe reads:

"Take 1 teaspoon black peppercorns, 1 whole nutmeg, 4 average sticks of cinnamon, 1 teaspoon coriander. These should all be pulverized in a mortar. About a handful each of de-stoned dates, dried figs, shelled almonds, and peanuts: chop these and mix them together. A bunch of cannabis Sativa can be pulverized. This along with the spices should be dusted over the mixed fruit and nuts, kneaded together. About a cup of sugar dissolved in a big pat of butter. Rolled into a cake and cut into pieces or made into balls about the size of a walnut, it should be eaten with care. Two pieces are quite sufficient."

So yes, cannabis can be eaten raw and this recipe is of no small historic importance. Unfortunately eating raw cannabis does lead to another problem – constipation – so it isn't really advisable.

Of course, the hippies love the recipe and it made its mark in the Peter Sellers film called, *I Love You Alice B Toklas.* The movie is centered on a lawyer who eats a hash brownie or two and then disappears from his wedding, running off to live with a hippie. These were depicted as real brownies and this is why the brownie became the food of choice to infuse cannabis into and this is how it became associated with Toklas, albeit erroneously.

As with any cannabis cooking, the secret to good pot brownies is experimentation though Some people use butter, while others choose peanut oil because it has a much higher smoke point than butter. To cut costs you can use leaves that have already been used in the production of bubble hash and, once you have rendered the THC into the fat, use a brownie mix in a box and just add it into the ingredients.

Cannabis is not limited to brownies, though! You can use it in a wide range of foods and if you go to any medical cannabis dispensary you will find a range of cookies, lozenges, fig bars, lollipops, and cakes. In fact, if you use it at home, you can use it in just about cooking you want, especially if you use it in the form of canna oil or cannabutter.

There are plenty of websites that are dedicated to cooking with cannabis and plenty of books, all of which give you, not just delicious recipes to try but a whole load of medical advice with it. That said, you don't need special recipes; just chuck it in your cooking and enjoy.

A couple of years ago, Roberta's Pizzeria in Bushwick held a hush-hush cannabis feast that made it into GQ magazine. They served a full gala meal that included cocktails with a cannabis base, a salad of vegetation that was grown on their roof and bluefish that was seasoned with canna oil and served in a cannabis yogurt sauce. Two different pizzas were served, both made from hempseed dough, seasoned with 'herbs' and pot pesto. And the desserts, way too numerous to mention, included vanilla tuille made with cannabutter, a hempseed crumble and a strawberry-rhubarb gelato that was served with cannabis cream.

Of course, this does pose one question – just how high can you get?

Chapter 3: Cannabis Extraction Methods

Cooking with cannabis is fun, a wonderful way to pep up your favorite recipes. However, it isn't just a case of crumbling a bud into your ingredients; you need to do a bit of planning first and that means learning the art of cannabis extraction. Cannabis contains something called THC, or tetrahydrocannabinol and this is soluble when you place it into an oil-based solvent. The THC is what is responsible for the feel-good factor of cannabis consumption but you cannot blend this straight into your cookie recipes. It has to be extracted first but, before you can do that, it needs to go through the act of decarboxylation.

This is a crucial part of using cannabis in food. To get the true value of the cannabis, it has to be heated up to a temperature that is not achievable in our digestive systems. There is a downside to this process – some of the aromatics that are responsible for the flavor and aroma will be lost. You can try adding raw material to the decarboxylated material in equal quantities but this is a matter for experimentation.

The Decarboxylation Process

Be warned – you will have an extremely strong cannabis smell throughout this process!

Once you have cured your buds they are ready for the decarboxylation process:

1. Preheat your oven to 225° F
2. Get a rimmed baking tray or an oven-safe dish and line it with parchment paper
3. Break the buds into small pieces and place them in an even layer in the tray or dish – do not overlap any but keep them close together
4. Bake in the preheated oven for about 20 minutes – this is to remove moisture so do keep an eye on them. The plant color should turn from a light to a dark brown shade and, when ready, should look crumbly
5. Set aside to cool and turn the heat in the oven to 240° F
6. Crumble the cooled cannabis bud evenly over the base of the dish and cover it with aluminum foil. Make sure to crimp the edges to create a tight seal
7. Bake for between 45 and 60 minutes
8. Remove and leave to cool off completely before you remove the foil
9. If the finished material is very fine you can use as is; if not, blend until fine but do not over blend – you don't want a fine powder
10. Store in a glass airtight container in a dry and cool place until you need it.

Infusion Methods

There are 3 main infusion methods to get your cannabis ready for use in your cooking:

Canna Oil

Ingredients:
- 6 cups of extra virgin olive oil
- 1 oz. fine ground cannabis bud

Instructions:
1. Use a double broiler or a heavy-bottomed pan to heat the oil slowly for a few minutes – the aroma of the oil will begin to appear
2. Add a little of the bud and stir to coat it; continue adding the bud slowly until it is all mixed in
3. Simmer for about 45 minutes on a low heat, stirring on occasion
4. Remove and cool before you strain it
5. Use a fine metal strainer and press the bud against it with a spoon to get all of the oil out of it
6. Recycle the used solids on the compost heap and store the oil in the refrigerator in an airtight container for up to 2 months

Cannabutter

Ingredients:
- ½ oz. decarboxylated cannabis bud
- 1 lb. unsalted butter
- 4 cups water

Instructions:
1. Cut the butter into small pieces and combine with the water and the cannabis bud in a pan
2. Heat over a low heat – do not boil, just simmer for 3 to 4 hours
3. Stir the mixture every half hour or so – it will begin to thicken so don't let it become too thick. The cannabis should be floating around 2 inches off the base of the pan and should never, ever, touch the base. If needed, add a little more water
4. After a few hours, the mixture should be dense, more compact and look glossy. Turn the heat off and leave to cool
5. Line a metal sieve with two cheesecloth layers, allowing some overhang
6. Pour the cooled mixture into the sieve, using a spatula to press it down into the cloth. Leave to drain over a bowl
7. Wearing gloves, bring the cheesecloth corners together and squeeze the butter out by twisting it
8. Discard the cannabis residue in the cloth and use a spatula to remove any butter left in the pan into the bowl
9. Refrigerate for about 2 hours until the butter has turned solid
10. When cooled, use a knife to separate the edges of the solidified butter and lift it from the bowl. Place it wet

side facing up onto a cutting board and mop off any excess water – expect your butter to have a slight green tinge to it

11. Store in an airtight container in the refrigerator until ready to use – do not keep for more than a couple of weeks

Canna Coconut Oil

Ingredients:
- ¼ to ½ oz. decarboxylated cannabis bud
- 1 cup organic coconut oil – use cold-pressed

Instructions:
1. Lay out a piece of 10 inches by 8-inch cheesecloth
2. Layer the cannabis evenly over a small area in the center of the cloth
3. Fold two opposite ends over to cover the cannabis
4. Fold one of the remaining open ends in, tuck it and roll the cloth
5. Tie the roll with cooking twine, making sure it is tight
6. Fill the bottom of a double broiler with a few inches of water and place the second pan on top
7. Turn the heat to medium – the water must reach a gentle boil, never a rolling boil
8. Put the coconut oil in the top pan. When it has melted almost completely, add in 1 cup of water, enough to cover the cannabis packet when you add it
9. Continue to heat until the oil is completely melted and then put the cannabis packet in. Press it down using the back of a spoon
10. Cover the broiler and leave cooking for about 90 minutes. Check on it every 30 minutes or so to make sure it is only boiling gently and that the water doesn't evaporate.
11. After about 90 minutes, the mixture of water and oil should be a deep green so turn the heat off and remove the cannabis packet; place it in a bowl and press it firmly with a spoon to get out any trapped oil.
12. When it has cooled off completely, you can squeeze it by hand as well

13. Add this oil to the rest and put it all in the refrigerator to cool off
14. When it has cooled, the water and the oil will separate – the oil should be a nice solid green color. Poke a couple of holes in it gently, place your hand over the top and drain the water off gently
15. Store in a glass airtight container until ready to use

Chapter 4: Cooking with Cannabis

Before you begin cooking with cannabis, you really need to understand the percentages of THC in the cannabis. On average, most cannabis strains have around 10% THC but all are different so make sure you find out what your strain percentage is. Let's say that you have 7 grams of cannabis or ¼ oz. Each gram of cannabis bud has a dry weight of 1000mg. If you have an average strain, with 10% THC, your THC weight would be 100 mg. As such, it would be safe to assume that, in terms of cooking 1 g of cannabis bud will have around 100 mg of THC in it.

Using this, you can find out how much TCH your particular strain of cannabis has per serving. Measure the ground cannabis and convert the measurement into milligrams. Divide that amount by the yield of the recipe to work out what the serving dose of THC is. Assuming you are making cookies, let's say an average recipe produces 60 cookies. You use 3 g of the cannabis which, divided by 10, is equal to 300 mg of THC. Divide that by the yield, in this case, 60, and you have 5 mg of THC per cookie.

Before you start cooking with cannabis, ensure that your kitchen area is properly prepped first. Use proper commonsense kitchen rules and be safe. Have a set of utensils and pans set aside purely or use in cooking with cannabis, to make sure there is no risk of cross-contamination and do make sure that your kitchen is well ventilated – this is an incredibly aromatic process!

A Note About Edibles

Eating cannabis with foods that are rich in fat and protein will ensure the cannabis effects last longer, whereas if you consume it in a candy or sugary form it won't last so long. Once you have consumed a cannabis edible, wait a period of 2 hours. If your high isn't there, don't be tempted to consume another edible – that will result in potential overdosing Simply eat something that is fatty to raise the cannabis effects. If you feel a bit too buzzed, drink a citric juice to bring your blood sugar up and counter the effects.

Cannabis Cooking Tips

The real secret to becoming a cannabis chef is practice. You will make mistakes and there will be disasters so before you get ready to cook for your guests, cast your eyes over these tips:

1. Remember that cannabis is fat-soluble; it is not water-soluble. For the THC to be released it has to be heated with fat, such as oil or butter.

2. Measure out the food you use in your recipes is important, just as it is in any recipe. You will more than likely have guinea pig testers so take it easy and use just ½ gram of THC per person.

3. Do not overheat your cannabis. Although heat is needed to release the THC, overheating can damage some of the cannabinoids. Cook for longer periods but at temperatures of below 330°F. Do NOT use the microwave!

4. Flavor is important so always test and be ready to improve on your recipes. Your cooking shouldn't have the single aim of creating a high; it should also taste nice too. Cannabis works a little like any normal herb – it will work with other herbs and, used in the form or oil or butter, is not overbearing.

5. Choose your moment for producing cannabis-infused cooking. Don't serve up a cannabis Christmas dinner, unless your guests are potheads! Ensure that your meal is served in a place where people can relax and enjoy what comes next

6. Do tell your guests what you will be serving them WELL AHEAD of time. Don't spring surprises on them because not everyone is receptive to using cannabis. Some people may even have adverse reactions to it or have certain food allergies or intolerances.

7. We know that, when eaten, cannabis can take an hour or two to have the desired effect. However, there will always be someone who can't wait for their high and will want more. This can be dangerous so make sure that every person is given a fair amount and never let anyone have a second portion

8. If a person reacts badly to cannabis ingestion, there are certain things you should do. Panic attacks or anxiety are best dealt with by leaving the person in a calm place, talking softly to them to tell them that the symptoms will disappear. The only other adverse effect that a person may experience is a sudden drop in blood pressure. They should be laid on the floor with their

knees raised up to above head level. If in doubt, call emergency services

9. Make sure you serve your cannabis meal in a relaxed atmosphere and have some good topics to hand for after-dinner conversation. Have the right music and soft drinks available for that inevitable thirst. Try to arrange it so that your guests stay overnight to avoid them driving under the influence.

10. Cannabis and alcohol don't mix very well so drink no more than one glass of wine with the meal – do not get drunk. Cannabis works very well with both coffee and chocolate so have these on hand for your guests.

Chapter 5: Cannabis Cookie Recipes

Marijuana Oatmeal Cookie Recipe

Ingredients:
- 8 ox canna oil or melted cannabutter
- 1 ¾ cup flour
- ¾ tsp baking powder
- ¾ tsp baking soda
- ¼ tsp nutmeg
- ½ tsp cinnamon
- ½ tsp salt
- 1 ½ cups soft brown sugar
- ¼ cup white sugar
- 2 eggs
- 2 tsp vanilla
- 1 cup chopped or whole raisins
- 3 ½ cups rolled oats

Instructions
1. Preheat your oven to 350° F
2. Whisk the flour, baking powder, baking soda cinnamon, nutmeg and salt together
3. Beat the butter or oil in a separate bowl with the sugar, vanilla, and eggs
4. Combine the dry and wet mixtures together and then add the oats and raisins. Stir until a smooth consistency is reached
5. Grease two cookie sheets and spoon out the dough in equal piles, about 3 inches apart. Press to flatten
6. Bake for about 7 to 10 minutes, until the cookies are brown
7. Remove from the oven and leave to stand for a couple of minutes before turning out onto a wire rack to cool

No-Bake Chocolate Cookies

Ingredients:

- 2 cups sugar
- ½ cup cannabutter
- ½ cup cocoa
- ½ cup milk
- 1 tsp vanilla
- ½ cup peanut butter
- 3 cups quick-cook oatmeal

Instructions:

1. Mix the cocoa, sugar, butter, and milk together in a saucepan and bring to the boil
2. Boil for one minute and then remove the pan from the heat. Stir the vanilla, peanut butter, and oatmeal in until combined
3. Drop spoonsful of the mixture onto greaseproof paper and leave to cool for at least half an hour before consuming

Cannabutter Cookies

Ingredients:
- 1 ½ cups all-purpose flour
- ½ cup white sugar
- ½ cup cornstarch
- 1 cup cannabutter

Instructions:
1. Preheat your oven to 375° F
2. Combine all the ingredients together until well mixed
3. Divide into balls of about 2 inches
4. Place the balls onto a greased cookie sheet and flatten with a fork
5. Bake until light brown, about 13 to 15 minutes and cool before serving

Cannabis Cinnamon Roll Cookies

Ingredients:

- 10 packs of cinnamon roll instant oatmeal
- 1 tsp baking soda
- 1 cup brown sugar firmly packed
- 2 cup cannabutter, softened
- 2 eggs
- 2 cups all-purpose flour
- ¼ cup water
- ¾ cup white sugar

Instructions:

1. Preheat your oven to 350° F
2. Mix both sugar with the butter until you have a creamy mixture
3. Beat the eggs in and add the baking soda and flour, mixing well to combine
4. Add the oatmeal packs and the water
5. Stir until the ingredients are evenly mixed to a cookie dough consistency
6. Make into small round balls and put onto a greased sheet
7. Bake for about 12 minutes or until golden brown
8. Transfer to a plate for cooling

Cannabis Ginger Cookies

Ingredients:

- 2 cups self-raising flour
- 2 tbsp. ground ginger powder
- ¾ tbsp. ground cinnamon
- ½ tbsp. ground cloves
- ¼ tsp salt
- ¾ cup cannabutter
- 1 cup white sugar
- 1 egg
- 1 tbsp. water
- 4 tbsp. molasses

Instructions:

1. Preheat your oven to 350° F
2. Sift the ginger, flour, baking soda, cloves, cinnamon and salt together
3. Cream the butter with the sugar in a separate bowl and beat the egg in. Add the molasses and water, and stir to mix
4. Add the dry ingredients gradually, stirring to combine
5. Spoon the mix onto plastic wrap and roll into a sausage shape
6. Leave for about 30 minutes to harden off
7. Slice the roll into rounds about 1 inch thick and place them onto an ungreased sheet, about 2 inches apart. Flatten each round a little
8. Back for about 8 to 10 minutes and then leave to cool for 5 minutes before transferring to a wire rack

Chocolate Peppermint Cannabis Crinkles

Ingredients:
- 4 oz. chopped unsweetened chocolate
- ¼ cup cannabutter
- 2 tsp instant coffee granules
- 1 ½ cups all-purpose flour
- ½ cup cocoa powder, unsweetened
- 2 tsp baking powder
- ¼ tsp salt
- 4 eggs
- 2 cups white sugar
- 1 tsp vanilla
- 12 oz. peppermint chips
- ½ cup powdered sugar

Instructions:
1. Heat a double broiler over water that is barely simmering and place the butter and chocolate into the top
2. Heat until both have melted, stirring constantly
3. Add the coffee, stir, and remove from the heat.
4. Stir the cocoa powder, flour, salt and baking powder together and set to one side
5. Mix the eggs, granulated sugar, and the vanilla together, beating to a light color
6. Fold the chocolate mix in and then add the rest of the dry ingredients (except for the powdered sugar), leaving the peppermint chips until last
7. Use plastic wrap to cover the dough and refrigerate for 2 hours or until the dough has firmed up
8. Preheat the oven to 325° F and grease two baking sheets
9. Sift the powdered sugar onto a plate or a small bowl

10. Divide the dough into balls of about ½ inch and then roll each ball in the sugar
11. Place the balls onto the sheets, 3 inches apart
12. Bake one tray for about 13 to 17 minutes or until the tops have crinkled and puffed – they cookies should feel firm to the touch. (Do not over bake)
13. Leave to cool while you bake the second sheet
14. Leave to cool for 5 minutes and transfer to a wire rack
15. For storage, place a slice of fresh bread in an airtight storage container with the cookies

Caramel Cannabis Cashew Cookies

Ingredients:

The Cookies:
- 2 tbsp. cannabutter
- 1/3 cup brown sugar, well packed
- 1 cup flour
- ¼ tsp salt

The Topping:
- ½ cup butterscotch chips
- 2 tbsp. cannabutter
- ¼ cup corn syrup
- 1 cup salted cashews

Ingredients:
1. Preheat your oven to 350° F
2. Blend 2 tbsp. of butter with the brown sugar until you have a crumb-like consistency
3. Add the salt and the flour and mix thoroughly
4. Press the mixture into an ungreased baking pan and bake for about 11 to 12 minutes
5. While the cookie mix is baking, melt the corn syrup and butterscotch with 2 tbsp. cannabutter – do not allow to boil
6. Pour the mixture over the cookie crust, add the cashews on top and leave to cool

Cannabis Peanut Butter Cookies

Ingredients:
- ½ cup cannabutter
- ½ cup peanut butter
- 1 cup sugar
- 1 ¼ cup flour
- ½ cup brown sugar
- 1 egg
- ½ tsp baking powder
- ½ tsp baking soda
- 1 tsp vanilla

Instructions:
1. Preheat your oven to 350° F
2. Melt the butter for a few seconds – it should not be hot or boiling
3. Mix with the peanut butter and then add ½ cup of flour
4. Mix well and add the brown sugar, half the white sugar, the egg, baking powder, baking soda, and vanilla; stir well to combine
5. Add the remaining flour and place the rest of the white sugar into a separate bowl
6. Shape the dough into balls and roll them in the sugar to coat
7. Place the balls onto a cookie sheet and bake for about 7 to 10 minutes, until they begin to crack on top and harden off
8. Remove from the oven and leave to cool.

Canna-Jam Cookies

Ingredients:

- 1 ½ cups flour
- 1/3 tsp baking powder
- 1/3 tsp salt
- ½ cup softened cannabutter
- ¾ cup white sugar
- 1 egg
- 1/3 tsp vanilla extract
- ½ cup powdered sugar
- 1 cup strawberry jam

Instructions:

1. Mix the flour, salt, and baking powder together and set to one side
2. Beat the butter with the sugar until fluffy and then beat the egg and vanilla in
3. Add the flour, beating to combine
4. Split the mixture into 2 and form into logs
5. Wrap the logs in plastic and leave for at least 60 minutes in the refrigerator
6. Preheat the oven to 350° F
7. Cut the dough logs into ¼ inch thick rounds and place them on cookie sheets
8. Bake until the edges are turning a golden-brown color, about 10 minutes
9. Transfer the cookies to a cooling rack and leave to cool
10. Place a tsp of jam onto a cookie and sandwich another cookie on top; repeat until all the cookies are used
11. Sprinkle with sugar before serving

Almond Canna-Cookies

Ingredients:
- 2 cups of sliced almonds
- 3 tbsp. all-purpose flour
- 1 tbsp. orange zest
- ¼ tsp salt
- ½ cup sugar
- 1/8 cup coconut oil
- ¼ cup canna coconut oil
- 2 tbsp. brown rice syrup
- 2 tbsp. full fat coconut milk
- 1 tsp vanilla
- ¼ cup of dark chocolate chips
- ¼ tsp coconut oil
- Powdered sugar

Ingredients:
1. Preheat your oven to 275° F
2. Line a couple of cookie sheets with parchment paper
3. Chop the almonds into smaller pieces and combine them with the flour, salt, sugar, and orange zest
4. Heat the oils, syrup and the coconut milk and stir until reaches a low boil; remove the pan from the heat and then add the vanilla, stirring it in
5. Add the dry ingredients gradually and then leave to cool for about 10 minutes, or until you can touch it
6. Spoon the mixture in rounds on the sheets leaving 3 or 4 inches between each one
7. Bake for about 15 to 17 minutes, turning the pan once during baking
8. Cool for 5 minutes before transferring to a cooling rack
9. Melt the chocolate chips in a double broiler and then drizzle the chocolate over the top using a fork; sprinkle powdered sugar on the cookies before cooking

Conclusion

Thank you again for purchasing this book!

I hope this book was able to help you to make your own Cannabis Extracts and Cookies and I truly hope you enjoyed the cookies, not just tasting them but making them too. Cannabis is no longer seen as the bad drug of yesteryear, at least not by everyone and it is fast becoming popular once more, as more and more places make medical cannabis legal.

Medical Marijuana

How to make Cannabis Oil:
All the Marijuana benefits and how to use
Marijuana for: anxiety, epilepsy, cancer, pain,
Tourette and more curing Cannabis uses.

Monica Jacobs

Table of Contents

Introduction

I want to thank you and congratulate you for downloading the book "How To Make Cannabis Oil: All The Marijuana Benefits".

This book contains a variety of information about medical benefits of marijuana, and includes detailed guide on how to make cannabis oil, which can be used to relieve pain and help patients in a variety of diseases.

We will start with the history, as all medication has a history and it is useful to understand why certain properties have been ignored, while others have been promoted. We will examine how Cannabis oil is made and developed for the use of medication and more specifically, this book will explore the various, identified maladies that cannabis has been – and is progressively – used to treat.

From acute anxiety related problems, to the controlling powers it contains for pain – even the acute pain cancer can serve up – cannabis is widely used and beneficial for the relief of many kinds of medical ailments.

For some it will be an education that demonstrates a distinct contrast to the image cannabis has endured over recent years. I hope the book will at least shine a light on an alternative source of relief. Maybe at the very least it will help readers to appreciate that cannabis is an amazing alternative to many invasive and poisonous painkillers that are currently, routinely used on suffering patients.

Thanks again for downloading this book, I hope you enjoy it!

Chapter 1 – Let's Weed out the History.

It may surprise a lot of readers to learn that Cannabis has been around for thousands of years. Of course it has, after all, it's just a plant. It may surprise some, because for many people – especially in Western society – one could well have been led to believe that the little green plant was somehow invented by those who wanted to get high on it's properties in the nineteen sixties. If we are to discover the history of Cannabis we must be ready to recognize that recent historical, mainstream opinion of this versatile *weed* has mainly been negative. It could well be argued that this is because the general public has largely been exposed to negative media insisting that for many years Cannabis was the devils way of making sure that your teenager went off the tracks. This view of Cannabis and the constant negative media attention has somehow created a negative smoke screen, lying directly in front of the plant, thus hiding some of the most useful medical applications of the drug.

There is no disguising the fact that marijuana plants are capable of producing a variation of drugs. As with most things we grapple with connected to the medical profession, it always depends on what your perspective is - whether a drug should be freely available - or if it should be hidden away, because somewhere along the timeline of history, someone has discovered that this particular drug is capable of being misused. In actual fact, this could be true of most drugs that are freely pumped into your veins, should you be unfortunate enough to need emergency medical help. It is unfortunate that Cannabis acquired such a poor reputation and we can probably attribute that fact to the ease to which the drug can be obtained and used as a mood changing substance.

The broader – some would say liberal - view is worth taking a look at, as Cannabis plants have been used for thousands of years by various different cultures as a legitimate medicine. There are three species of the cannabis plant and these species also include seven sub-species. Each species – and sub-species - of the cannabis plant contains a variation of properties and it is for this reason that cannabis can be rightly judged as being incredibly versatile when it comes to medical uses.

As is the case with many plants with leaves growing from them, cannabis was often used as a tea based therapy. It is best known – in terms of ancient use – as the herb, that when crushed and used as a tea drink, it will then be utilized as a useful painkiller. Hemp is just one category of cannabis and was used extensively in the ancient world as an element that was high in protein and therefore, could be used for a variety of food and fiber products. Hemp is cannabis – as it is one variety – and yet it does not contain the elements within to include itself among the much feared – by many in the general population – hallucinogenic category of cannabis derivatives.

As hemp was being used around the ancient world as a food source, it was only a matter of time before other such plants related to it were being experimented with as possible sources of medical aid. It was the practice of many ancient cultures to experiment with plants. It stands to reason that if one cannot simply run to the pharmacy to get relief for ones ills, then the next best thing is to experiment with what nature has supplied.

China was the first known nation to experiment with the medical uses of cannabis. Even as far back as records of such things were kept, cannabis derivatives were discovered in some cases to have the hallucinogenic qualities and were subsequently regarded as a drug that needed some careful monitoring and usage. In those days it was more likely that your doctor would have warned you against taking too many painkillers – cannabis – in case it caused you to see visions of demonic forces. However, cannabis remained a useful antidote for pain of various kinds. The message quickly spread and it wasn't long before the powerful pain killing properties of cannabis were spread from China, reaching the furthest parts of Asia, as well as Africa and the Middle East.

Maybe it is because the Western societies of the world were not exposed to these medical benefits within ancient culture that has made it more difficult for modern Western society to fully appreciate the painkilling properties available from harvesting cannabis? Asian and African cultures however, quickly realized that there were more benefits that could be gleaned from cannabis. Eventually, more and more imagination went into the usages of cannabis. Soon a kind of paste made from the buds and leaves of certain cannabis plants were made into a substance that was to become named, bhang. There are historical records of ancient Indian cultures now discovering that *bhang* was producing another beneficial antidote for the communities unable to find relief elsewhere but from herbs and plants. This new discovery was that bhang was useful and now being widely used to treat that most widespread of human plagues, *anxiety*.

As you can imagine, the drink that helped with anxiety was destined to become popular. The beneficiaries of all the various different forms and varieties with which cannabis was now widely being used, bragged of depressing symptoms dissipating as they drank their rather odd tea. Some of the earliest recorded maladies for which cannabis as a form of paste, or tea remedied were, as an anti-depressant, an aid to concentration, a powerful potion to rid one of excessive flatulence and one that would rid him whom was full of phlegm from his bunged up state.

Medieval medicine, as you can imagine, was in a lot of ways quite brutish. However, in India, Hemp became revered, in Egypt, cannabis was being used to treat inflammation, China were now ensconced in the widespread use of different species of the cannabis plant and there are records – 200 BCE - that record the use of cannabis as an anesthetic. A perfectly ground drink was concocted from the cannabis plant, converted into a powder and then added to wine, became the perfect answer for surgeons when they had to knock people out.

Different parts of cannabis plants were being experimented upon as time led up to what we would describe as *modern day.* It remained the domain of Asian countries to continue to experiment with the cannabis plant and as a result, a great list of maladies was increasingly cited as those whereby cannabis could intervene. It is reported that blood clots were eased with the use of cannabis oil; tapeworms could apparently be removed and if you were afraid of your hair disappearing with old age, cannabis oil could even help you with that.

The Middle East joined in the cannabis party in the latter half of the medieval era many Muslims could now smoke *hashish* – the Arab word for marijuana. The popularity of cannabis throughout the Arab communities was such that, just as throughout Asia, Muslim communities were valuing cannabis as a powerful aid in medicine.

There were always to be times of questioning the validity of the cannabis plant as a useful tool for medicine, many cultures calling for care to be used when applying the term *medicine* as one of it's attributes. In the countries that allowed cannabis and medicine to merge and flourish, we have had reports – some modern day – of remarkable inroads into cannabis use becoming more *at one* with science within medicine. This was something that did not happen so much in the West and so, the reports of cannabis being used and genuinely making groundbreaking progress in the treatment of various strains of cancer, and jaundice, were being somewhat ignored by what was now regarded as *the developed world*.

We will discover more of the history behind this fascinating little plant in subsequent chapters that will deal with the use of cannabis in specific areas of medicine.

Chapter 2 – What in the World is a Cannabinoid?

Cannabis contains *components*, or *properties, which* are referred to as cannabinoids. There are in access of 450 different components available within the cannabis family and this means that there are myriad different properties that can be used for the treatment of various different ailments and complaints, all acting upon the nervous system in a slightly different way. 66 – some researchers argue this figure is nearer to 85 - of these components are officially classed as cannabinoids – not all of the components have this classification. These cannabinoids are unique to the cannabis plant. One of the most well known – due to the amount of research available – is delta-9-tetrahydrocannabinol. The reason this cannabinoid is probably the best known of the active ingredients within a cannabis plant, is due to the fact that it is the element most responsible for the psychoactive – mood changing – effects of the cannabis family of plants.

This *active* ingredient of cannabis is most commonly known as THC. The *other* components inherently found within the cannabis plant react with THC and to some extent water-down the effects of THC if ingested by human beings – and other animals. Therefore, it is estimated that the cannabis plant regulates itself by enabling the components within the plant to act upon the cannabinoids, ensuring that the strength of the psychoactive effects are somewhat modified.

Active cannabinoids are classed by being separated into subclasses of which we can still refer too as active cannabinoids. These subcategories are usually better known by their abbreviations and for ease of clarification I will not confuse the reader with a whole list of scientific names. However, the terms commonly used are as such: CBG, CBC, CBD, THC, CBN, CBDL. When one is exploring the usage and usefulness – for the purposes of medical relief – these abbreviated initials when trying to identify active ingredients present in a cannabis product will always confront the seeker of medical relief. The most common active ingredients within a cannabis product are the cannabinoids, THC and CBD.

Cannabinoids simply interact with the receptors located within the central nervous system, much the same as any substance that can be classified as an opiate. This is where the reputation for 'getting high' has come from and yet; it is noteworthy to examine the fact that other opiate based chemicals, such as morphine will be used quite openly within a pain critical situation for medical purposes – rendering the patient just as *high* in terms of psychological mood changed. The byproduct of the cannabinoids will react with the central nervous system in just the same way in which many other, more *recognized* and accepted substances will. This pain barrier action is largely lost on some medical professionals, mainly due to the *bad name*, via *negative media coverage*, given to cannabis use.

CBD is the most commonly known and used cannabinoid. CBD is usually, up to forty percent present in cannabis resin. As this is the most common way in which cannabis is used as a recreational drug, it is understandable why it has been somewhat overlooked as a legitimate pain killing substance. The ironic fact about CBD is that it is non-psychoactive. This may come, as somewhat of a shock to many cannabis recreational users, however it is the THC value of the cannabis plant that is known to react more readily with the central nervous system. It is the high value THC marijuana that is likely to be most sought after by the seasoned recreational user, but it is the high value CBD cannabis that has caught the eye of the medical professional.

We have established that (CBD) Cannabidiol and (THC) tetrahydrocannabinol are the two principle elements we are interested in the marijuana plant. These two cannabinoids act quite differently when we consider the possible use they may be to the medical profession. As THC is very much more psychoactive than CBD, it is CBD that interests scientists working upon different ways in which cannabis plants might benefit the ailing patient. CBD is unique inasmuch as it cannot actually create the recreational *high* so sought after by the recreational user of cannabis.

Doctors and those working upon ways in which cannabis can be used in medicine, are working so hard with CBD cannabis derivatives because it has less side effects that other strains of cannabis. Through the years cannabis per se has been largely ignored and regarded as the bad boy of medicine. Now however, children are being able to be treated with high content CBD substances. Anxiety related illnesses are also high on the scientist's agenda and we will look at this a little closer in a later chapter of this book. It has always been the psychoactive effects of marijuana that has held it back medically. Now, with a more sophisticated body of medical experts those days seem to be consigned – thankfully – to history.

One of the most ironic discoveries concerning the use of cannabis cannabinoids in the field of medicine is that rather than *formally* being hailed as a major contributor of psychosis, certain CBD strains of the plant are now being considered as substantial contributors to the field that is trying to find more affective **anti**psychotic drugs. Notwithstanding the fact that many THC based products may yet be identified as having a negative long-term effect upon the individual users psychological wellbeing. The latter negative theory may in fact have been the very barrier stopping researchers from exploring further. It is pleasing to realize that science has advanced further than ever, inasmuch as it is willing to search deeper to find the truth out about cannabis, rather than judging it's merits, solely based on the aforementioned negative press. If THC derivatives are proved to have a long-term negative effect upon psychosis, as evident within individual users of the drug, then CBD products look like possibly making up for this discrepancy. The antipsychotic effect of certain CBD products are now known to reduce the negative effect of psychosis within THC users, as well as starting to make a considerable contribution to the overall research into the use of antipsychotic drugs. This discovery could mean that very soon, doctors will be seriously thinking about using CBD products in their combat with a host of different disabling psychological symptoms found in their patients.

Chapter 3 – Cannabis Oil.

Cannabis oil is an entity within itself, when we are taking about the use of cannabis for recreational use, or indeed the use of cannabis *extracts* for use within the medical field. Oil extracted from the cannabis plant is a very concentrated formulation of the elements within cannabis. It is recognized already as a useful treatment for ailments such as cancer, and other chronic illnesses. We will look at these specific illness treatments in later chapters, but for now we will explore how cannabis oil is made.

Cannabis is cannabis, is cannabis, is a very misleading opinion to hold – which is why it is the subject of extensive medical research. There are many different plants, strains and as we discovered in the previous chapter, different elements therein that will react in different ways, within differing sets of environments and conditions. This is why it is advisable to take the time to carry out extensive research before embarking on producing your own cannabis oil product. The end product will be only as effective as the time and effort you have taken to choose the correct method of production. The other warning to would be producers of cannabis oil, is that each compound will be effective in the treatment of only a select number of different medical conditions. If you put the time in and research the correct combination of elements however, there is no reason why effective remedies cannot be produced. An example of what we are exploring here is that even the choice of *organic* cannabis to use within your cannabis oil concoction may be preferable, as poorly operating immune systems can be effected by pesticides, insecticides and fertilizers used to grow cannabis.

The combination of oils rich in THC and CBD – see previous chapter – are thought to work well with certain illnesses and yet, they are less effective than combinations that are high in CBD and low THC. Chemical compounds that contain an abundance of elements from other plants as well as cannabis are also thought to be more effective than compounds that just contain cannabis plant extracts. The warning to all those seeking medical help, is ask someone who knows what they are doing, or do your own research when you are seeking help making a cannabis oil compound for a particular illness. You do not want to end up using a cannabis oil that is not helpful, or worse, has a negative effect upon your wellbeing.

If you are planning on creating your own strain of cannabis oil you will need a good deal of paraphernalia. Again, putting all the correct materials needed together is quite a skill in itself, so if you can find someone who has made cannabis oil themselves, you might want to learn from any reported mistakes they made, before embarking on this activity yourself. If you are planning to work indoors while making cannabis oil you will need to ensure you have good ventilation in the room you are working.

Your oil will need to be produced from approximately one ounce of very high quality medical cannabis. Search for the cannabis that has been produced to compliment your particular medical needs. Only use cannabis that has been produced for medical purposes. There are a number of kitchen utensils you will need and again check that you are working to a recipe that is only catering for specific medical needs in mind. Everclear alcohol is required during the process and can be obtained freely on-line. High-proof alcohol that will burn off without leaving toxic residue is highly recommended. The other essentials are: a cooker similar or the same as a rice cooker, a mixing bowl, the obligatory cooking wooden spoon and spatula, a large container in which to catch excess liquid, some oral syringes – remember they must be sterile. You will need a cloth that is able to act as a straining utensil – a ladies stocking may suffice. The last piece of equipment to have ready before you begin is parchment paper.

Before you begin to make your oil you must ensure that you are not working in a cluttered environment where there are lots of hazards. The last thing you will want is a major fire occurring when you apply heat during the process; so ensure you have a lot of space to work in and there isn't anything lying around that is likely to catch fire easily. If you are particularly in need of a red warning sign before you begin, it may be in the fact that the worst that can happen during the process of making your oil is that you will create an explosion. You will be heating up flammable material, so create lots of space, check the ventilation again and make sure there is nothing on the floor that you may slip on or trip on. Basically, you are working with volatile substances that should be respected throughout the process. Latex gloves and a fire extinguisher might be handy to have close to hand. I am not exaggerating the possible obstacles that may be forthcoming if I suggest also, that you wear a safety mask, for the fumes and a pair of goggles to reduce the risk of splash-back burns.

Please be assured, this is not a recipe necessarily intended to be followed without further research. We are investigating the theory of how cannabis oil can be produced, rather than a practical guide. However if you are knowledgeable about such arts as using high temperatures safely methods and how to handle toxic substances, you could use this guide to produce cannabis oil.

Now that we have secured a safe environment for ourselves we can start the process of creating cannabis oil.

You will need to place your cannabis oil into your bowl and pour just enough alcohol on top of it to cover the ounce of plant material. Mixing the cannabis with the alcohol – use the wooden cooking spoon – will cause the cannabis to merge its precious cannabinoids with the alcohol fluid. Then you will need to utilize that woman's stocking we listed earlier, as your fluid will need to be strained, before the whole process of mixing the alcohol – new alcohol – with the cannabis is repeated. This process is carried out so that the maximum extract from your cannabis.

The next part of the process involves using the extra mixing bowl or separate container to **catch** the mulch you have produced. It will need to be carefully strained again through another stocking and into the second container. You will need to take care as bits can easily drop away and need to be directed into the bowl via the straining stocking. When you have strained all you can into a second container, squeeze the stocking out over the bowl used to catch the alcohol / cannabis mulch, to ensure that your entire cannabis product is nicely saved into the second bowl.

The soaking and merging of alcohol with cannabis mulch is not over yet. You have removed and captured most – but not all - of the valuable cannabinoids from your mixture. What is needed now is that the entire process is repeated to ensure all of the cannabinoids are captured in the mixture by means of being removed from the cannabis, by mixing with the alcohol. Therefore, pour your cannabis into your first mixing bowl and repeat the process of soaking in alcohol and straining into the second bowl.

This whole process is to extract the cannabinoids from the cannabis – as this is the basis of your forthcoming oil. Then you will need to burn off the alcohol.

You are then left with a dark green substance in your second mixing bowl, having been soaked, mixed, and strained **twice.**

Now we need to burn off the alcohol, removing it from the cannabis mulch you have created. Here is where the heat is applied and where you take one more look that the room is ventilated, you are wearing your mask – at the very least. You ideally need all the fumes of this heating process to be ventilated outside. You can use any small stew, slow, or rice cooker basin to start to burn off the alcohol from your cannabis mulch.

The reason that using a rice cooker is probably the safest option is that you can easily remove it if the temperature rises too quickly and you think that safety measures dictate that you remove it to a location outside of the area you are working. You need to fill the cooker bowl until it is about three quarters full of alcohol, once you have the cannabis in the bottom of the cooker bowl. **Leave the lid off.** If you have any cheesecloth, it is helpful to drape over the top of the bowl – it stops grit, and dust entering the mix. Always ensure the cloth does not make contact with the oil mixture.

Let the alcohol boil off and top it up if the levels get too low. What you are waiting for is a thick, dark green substance to start to form at the bottom of your cooking bowl. Remove the bowl from heat when you start to see bubbles – that have been rising in the mix throughout - start to subside. You need to continually mix the pot, looking for the absence of bubbles.

You can now take away your **oil** from the bottom of the cooking bowl. This is best attempted with spatula – see materials needed above. The oil mixture should be thick and dark green before you attempt to remove it from the bowl. The parchment paper comes in handy here, as the oil can be transferred safety – using the spatula – from cooking bowl to parchment paper. If your oil is nice and thick, you will probably need to use a toothpick to remove it all. It is a slow and intricate process, so if you are the impatient type, take a breath and decide not to rush. The best oil will need to be literally scraped of the bottom of the cooking bowl.

If you have used a double cooker burning technique, you need to fill the bottom of your double cooking pan with boiling water, then add the alcohol to the top pan, so that it is only alcohol that makes contact with the cannabis.

Don't let your pans boil over, by allowing the cooking pan – which ever option of pan you use – to remain taking on more heat once it is boiling; rather, let it simmer for about 20 minutes. If the liquid ceases to simmer, apply more heat to keep the boiling bubbles coming. Whatever **cooking pan** option you use, you are still only looking for one result. That final result will be about three quarters of a pan of alcohol and cannabis substance boiling for about 20-25 minutes until the alcohol burning off leaves a thick oily resin at the base of the pan.

Why did we need syringes? This is an ideal way of dosing your cannabis oil. Suck up equal measures of oil into the syringes, and you will know that you have equal measures to dispense later.

It is highly advisable to look at the many videos online that outline how to produce cannabis oil whatever cooking utensil you choose to use. There are always pitfalls with all methods and you may find that first attempts can be disappointing. Remember, safety first.

Chapter 4 – Anxiety Disorders & CBD.

We can now take a look at some of the specific medical disorders that medical marijuana has proved to be very effective at alleviating.

We will look at many more uses of medical marijuana in chapter 5 however, it is believed that more than 50% of all people who reach for marijuana for medical purposes, do so because of anxiety related problems, therefore, we will be giving this subject some priority.

Cannabis is now thought to be especially reliant when it comes to relieving the symptoms of certain manifestations of many differing types of **anxiety disorder.** There will always be healthy debate and there are equally always those who may choose to stick to old historical – or media – determination – that is usually a wholly negative response - as to the uses of cannabis when treating anxiety, as well as other medical disorders.

The problem with analyzing the usage of marijuana is that, as we have discovered ourselves there are so many different strains and chemical compounds to be found in the vast array of cannabis substances available; it is incredibly hard to collect data from users of cannabis who all use the same strain or type of cannabis product. We have also discussed in this book how important it is to treat particular disorders with the correct amounts and combinations of cannabis cannabinoids. The long-term use of **any** painkilling substance is highly likely to bring along certain uncomfortable side effects.

If you have ever been prescribed painkillers, when you read the – sometimes extensive – material that comes within the packaging, you will usually find that a good deal of that information is there to warn you against the long-term use or side effects of the drug prescribed. Therein lays the problem with opinion concerning the long-term use of marijuana. Any drug – when abused – will likely cause you some physical or psychological damage, however, what we are going to look at in this book are the positive situations that lead us to believe that, if used correctly, certain mixes, strains, etc. can indeed be incredibly helpful to the suffering patient.

The positive arguments toward cannabis being used for medical treatments – medical marijuana – is that there is overwhelming historical evidence that civilizations and cultures worldwide have used certain strains of the marijuana plant to treat all sorts of illnesses, including those that effect the anxiety levels within individual patients.

It is the American Academy of pediatrics that is currently leading the way in terms of research into the use of the herb for medical reasons, however, once again, due to the lack of scientific proof, despite their believe in the *results* medical marijuana bring, they too are unwilling to step forward and say definitely that it acts as consistently as other medication.

It is the cannabinoid CBD – see chapter 2 – that is thought to be most helpful for the treatment of anxiety. This knowledge alone, if it were more positively shared, would direct those with anxiety disorders to a more appropriate cannabis combination – as users of the drug. The cannabinoid element of the cannabis plant, acts in the same way as many painkillers currently, widely and without needing a defense do. The chemical compounds within the CBD strain of cannabis, act upon the receptors in the brain that are responsible for producing the chemicals / hormone action in the body that is responsible for how we feel.

We have discussed in this volume that the cannabinoid CBD does not act upon the brain causing a psychoactive response. In other words, it does not cause one to become *high* if ingested into the system. It is this cannabis rich in CBD that is thought to be so effective when treating many people that suffer with depression and related illnesses. The problem with CBD research is that the cannabinoid THC needs to be used differently – as it is also useful when treating certain **other** ailments - and the clear distinction between the use of CBD and THC based substances needs to be clearly stated.

As CBD rich cannabis has little or no side effects and does not act on the brain to cause a psychological high therefore, it needs to be carefully used for the actions with which it specializes to counteract. A patient may in fact *become* over anxious and present as a patient suffering from anxiety disorder. If, upon discovering that one of the causes of the malady has been induced by the overuse of cannabis rich in THC, then, it is a fact that CBD rich cannabis treatments have been found to be extremely active in counteracting this malady.

Cannabis is too complex a plant, containing too many variations of chemical compounds to simply label as one thing or another – in terms of benefits to health. The point that needs to be purposely advocated by those who understand the correct use of certain cannabis chemical compounds is this; if the correct cannabinoids are used to treat the correct ailments, within the field of medical marijuana, then we can then begin to discover new and exciting uses for this multifaceted little plant, rather than continually struggle with the concept that if certain compounds cause a psychological reaction – similar to morphine – it should be dismissed as a medicine altogether. There remains a distinct nervousness among the researching medical world regarding the use of cannabis in medication. There is also a growing feeling of frustration among a massive – and growing number – of active marijuana users, because they are indeed using compounds within the vast array available, that are bringing relief to their maladies with considerable effectiveness.

CBD rich cannabis is fast becoming known as the anti-inflammatory, anti-pain, anti-**anxiety** drug of choice for so many people around the world that it will soon become impossible to ignore the powerful remedies it can provide for people. We must not – for one minute dismiss the effectiveness of THC rich cannabis compounds, because as research does strive forward, all that is essentially being discovered is that this particular strain of cannabis is considerably useful for a range of other ailments that CBD rich compounds are less or ineffective to help relieve.

If we consider the fact that certain ailments sometimes require chemical compounds that do indeed act on the brain causing a psychoactive response – feeling a psychological high - such as the way mainstream painkillers for chronic conditions are used throughout the medical profession currently – I have already cited morphine as an ideal example - we must also consider more closely that the cannabis compounds rich in the cannabinoid THC must also be considered as a powerful alternative to some of the drugs currently on the market – and making the pharmaceutical giants very rich indeed. THC cannabis compounds have been identified as being extremely effective when used slightly differently than those rich in CBD. Those illness cited have been in cases where severe pain is a constant threat to the quality of life offered to certain suffering patients, when severe inflammation needs to be reduced, when seizures need to be controlled, to name but a few. We will go on now to discover how the use of medication using elements of the cannabis plant, help people in their battle against cancer and the inevitable pain that this malady brings with it.

Chapter 5 – Medical Marijuana & the Bigger Picture.

One might be forgiven for being slightly confused because of the many different references to cannabis, cannabinoids, and marijuana, throughout the course of this book. I have chosen this section of the book to add some clarification, as it is probably the case that you have picked up this book because you may be thinking about using medical marijuana to aid you with a medical malady – or at least to explore whether it might be useful as a general aid to muscle fatigue, and or pain. We have looked at the history – which has been a history of extensive use of marijuana to ease medical symptoms for centuries. We have also looked at the theory and complexities of how one might be able to produce their own cannabis oil. It is likely that **now** is the time that you are near to making a decision about whether the use of this effective and versatile drug. If you have had no exposure to the use of marijuana up until this point in your life – which is likely if you have downloaded this volume – now is the time you need to learn about the intricacies of the drug itself and the many uses it has.

This chapter will attempt to widen the argument for the use of medical marijuana for various illnesses and painful symptoms. I will cover all of the main illnesses, whereby medical marijuana has proved – to a greater or at least more positive degree - to be effective. I will highlight the illnesses and / or symptoms where medical marijuana has proved to be particularly effective – upon first mention of it - so that the reader may be able to spot them easily.

To clarify, cannabis plants are the species of plant that produce the – hopefully - large buds, which later become dried through a process of delicately rearing the biggest cannabis plants - with the aim to produce the biggest buds. These cannabis buds can grow in varying degrees of size, with the biggest of them to be larger than a fist. The cannabis plant's buds can be dried and then referred to as, **buds of marijuana**. We have covered cannabinoids which contain specific and quite complex compounds that are to be found in each individual species and therefore, also in the differing buds of marijuana. There are many different species of the cannabis plant and as we are discovering, each different plant has the capacity to produce different elements and chemical compounds that can be used within the field of medical marijuana.

Marijuana has been a feature of what the modern day pharmacist may refer to as, herbal remedies for many centuries. The term herbal remedy can be slightly misleading, as it tends to reduce the validity of the product – in the eyes of the medical profession – as that which is more a case of hit and miss treatment, using whichever herbs and plant species that happen to be available at the time. The truth about the ancient use of this powerful plant is somewhat more sophisticated than modern medicine may still give it credit for. It may surprise the reader to learn that many modern day medicines derive their origins from plants, e.g. aspirin – from willow bark – and penicillin – from penicillin mold, to name just two.

Many drugs are what may be regarded as synthetically produced by various methods of laboratory techniques. The problem cannabis is currently experiencing is that the detailed studies and research that has been - and is now being - carried out, is still in its infancy compared to many other drugs currently used in modern medicine. This fact causes many users of cannabis substances to be rather frustrated, as they are aware that the drug can be effectively used for the purpose of pain relief and other medical problems, but as it is largely viewed with a great deal of suspicion by those who are still desperately trying to catch up with the research needed to award the drug with the equivalent of a parole award – after many years of medical imprisonment – inflicted upon it by medical researchers.

What is known and what we have already discovered is that the *different compounds* within the cannabis plant, can aid *different types* of physical and psychological malady. This fact is important, as if the wrong strain of cannabis compound is used for an incompatible illness, the results will be disappointing.

The cannabinoid THC is reported to be particularly effective when used to treat, **acute pain**, such as is experienced with diseases such as **cancer.** It is also very good at relieving **nausea**. Let us consider for a moment the severe nature of nausea and vomiting when patients are undergoing cancer treatments. **Chemotherapy-related nausea** is incredibly severe, just as radiation therapy nausea is. The THC compound found within certain THC cannabis plants is reported to be the single most effective reliever of such horrendous bouts of nausea. The reason this drug is vilified is mainly due to the fact that THC type cannabis produces the much-celebrated *side effect* of a psychoactive *'high'*. The question that many people are asking is this. If drugs such as morphine – that are also highly addictive – are freely used in the attempt to ease the pain of cancer patients, then why isn't cannabis – which produces a similar effect, but still leaves one comparatively conscious? Morphine tends to knock you out quite rapidly and yet, there seems to be a resistance by some medical professionals to recognize medical marijuana as a legitimate drug that can ease the pain of many people who may be terminally ill?

Many people use cannabis to ease the pain of cancer related treatments or pain that is related to the pressure that the body is called to experience when it is fighting the invasion of a tumor. Unfortunately, many of these people have to break the law in order to gain relief. If the correct dosage of cannabis rich in THC was to be monitored and applied to the suffering patient accordingly, the question remains – after considerable proof of the effectiveness of THC cannabis use among those who suffer from cancer – why isn't cannabis recognized as a viable and legitimate drug for the use of treating cancer and related symptoms?

If medical marijuana was introduced as a viable and legal option for those who need treatment of pain related illness, many more inroads could be researched as to how best to administer the correct strain and dosage of cannabis, to meet the needs of the patient. If we examine this medical option further, we discover that it is important to look at how marijuana is ingested into the body. If it is taken orally, the absorption into the system is much slower than when the drug is smoked or vaporized and inhaled. However, the oral option means that the effects of the drug may last longer and if inhaled, the drug could very well meet the needs of many who present at hospitals in a great deal of pain. The truth of the matter is that the research needed to introduce the drug into mainstream medical practice is still wholly lacking in depth and so the specific uses of cannabis are still known only to those who use the drug.

The very fact that medical marijuana is so celebrated, due to the positive effect it has upon nausea, led a number of patients to seek it out when the world went through the horrendous experience, that was the introduction of a new disease in the 1980's. **A.I.D.S. and the myriad illnesses** and painful symptoms it brought along with it, caused many people to immediately find solace with the knowledge that medical marijuana was particularly good at ceasing nausea pangs experienced by the patients. During the time of the explosion of A.I.D.S. related deaths, many patients found that not only did it stop the constant rush to hang over the toilet seat, but it also gained great acclaim for also killing the painful symptoms caused by the **gradual, internal breakdown of the body's system**. The research into why the drug was so effective however, hit a very hard brick wall once it was established that the drug was so helpful, alas, the reason once again was due to the controversial nature of the reputation attached to *cannabis*.

There are however, still many suffering patients that use cannabis oil for relief, even though the disease seems now to be better controlled and it is out of the searching eye of the media. This reluctance to continually publicize the positive effects of cannabis oil treatment on those who are in pain has left the victims having to undergo the indignity of searching for the substance in many areas of the world where cannabis is still deemed to be illegal.

Another breakthrough discovery when studying the use of medical marijuana on patients that suffer from diseases that include uncomfortable wasting symptoms such as, **weight loss and muscle wasting**, was to be found within wider investigation of it's uses. The use of cannabis oil often caused patients to gain a more healthy appetite. The effects of this knowledge may be obvious, but the benefits of helping patients not to go down the spiral effect of continually losing weight, not only helped with the general robustness that patients could more easily maintain, it also helped by encouraging the ***body's immune system to gain strength.*** This multiple benefit is an incredible piece of medical muscle because if a patient is eating and not losing so much weight then the body is far more able to heal.

It is well known that cannabis, when it is inhaled, can be extremely effective when ***neuropathic pain*** is present in a patient. Neuropathy pain is caused when certain cancer treatments – such as chemotherapy – cause damage to the nerves. The nerves that are affected are those controlling movement – in the arms and legs. The many neurological conditions that cannabis oil in particular can relieve are many and varied.

Cannabis oil has also proved to be incredibly effective for those who suffer from ***epilepsy.*** Doctors are inundated with information – from patients – that suggest that when medical marijuana is applied to those who have regular seizures, they find that the sedation properties of the drug causes a distinct ***decrease in the amount of seizures*** they experience.

There are many anecdotal reports that suggest regular but controlled use of medical marijuana can significantly reduce seizures. As a result of this fact, many clinical studies were carried out – over the last 20 years – and there was indeed a serious attempt by the medical profession to introduce it as a legitimate form of treatment. What the studies failed to do was to determine which elements of the various cannabis strains were best at reducing seizures. One study that included 48 people to go through clinical trials were found to be ingesting too many variations of the drug. The results were therefore inconclusive. Those patients that were found to be relieving their symptoms with high value THC cannabis oil were all found to be in a position whereby their seizures were dramatically reduced by its properties. Federal regulations banned any further clinical trials thereafter.

Let us now consider the distressing symptoms of **Tourette syndrome.** This is at last one area of medicine when it seems that the medical profession agree with its suffering patients. This is probably because they are in considerable disarray. There are very few options open to clinicians when they are faced with patients with Tourette's. The malady is one that causes the patient to present with what is commonly termed as 'nervous ticks'. 'Ticks' can present in many different forms – the most reported ones are the uncontrollable urge to unleash verbal volley's of abuse, that are often deemed as inappropriate behavior, especially in a public place. The other manifestation of a 'tick' is the uncontrollable movement of certain muscles and nervous reactions, which could range from slight twitching movements to seemingly violent – not intentionally – movement of any part of the body. The lack of *mainstream* medical breakthroughs available for this malady has almost pushed the medical profession into the admission that the only viable option for many patients is medical marijuana.

Medical analysis *is* actually available for this condition and it is believed that clinical tests carried out over the last fifteen years have indicated that those suffering from this dreadful malady do respond well when using medical marijuana. If it true that medically controlled use of marijuana for this condition has proved to be effective, you may be asking why it is yet to be recognized as a legitimate drug by certain government agencies who persist in the notion that all marijuana use is sinister and so must remain illegal? Good question.

Tourette troubles very few people and it is reported that it is close to only 1% of the entire population – who are actually counted in these reports – worldwide who suffer. The troubling thing for researchers is that it is still unknown what actually causes the syndrome. This may account for why there is no known guaranteed cure, but as it has been proved that sufferers respond to medical marijuana, this may increase the pressure upon federal government, to simply let people access it freely.

We have been able to touch only the very pinnacle of a very large iceberg that exists within the debate about which medical maladies we can use medical marijuana for. The existing information that is to be found by researching the extensive body of the iceberg of knowledge still lies largely beneath the surface of the water. If you are asking – by downloading this book – *how do I use medical marijuana* – the answer is quite simple.

Once you have established the particular area – illness or pain – you want to address, the ideal way of finding out which strain of cannabis, and which *form* the marijuana you acquire needs to be presented in, is this. We have discovered over the course of this small book many different types, strains and formulas marijuana can be produced in and we have linked certain strains – such as the CBD and the THC rich types of cannabis – to certain types of maladies.

As there are so many different strains of the cannabis plant, I have only included the most abundant and commonly used types of cannabis. If you have read the information and even tried to use certain types of cannabis to aid your fight against illness or pain and you haven't yet found relief, you have some options ahead of you. The legitimate use of any forms of cannabis will very much depend on where you live. It is very much scorned upon in the U.K. and yet there are many *health* stores in the U.S. where the request for cannabis oil can often be an indication that you are in fact suffering from an illness that requires it's properties. There are many heath stores in the U.S. that supply cannabis oil on the assumption that it is for medical use with no questions asked. My advice would be, be wise and do some research, as to where you can acquire the product, before you decide upon where you will buy it from. The U.S. is making great strides in its ability to let go of the old cliché reputation of cannabis, and so research, research, research.

I have just accessed an article quite freely available on-line that has described one mans elation because he had found cannabis oil supplied from a health store in the ***U.K.*** The owner of the store understood that the man has cancer and the headline reads, 'A Drop at a Time: How Cannabis Oil is Changing the Lives of Cancer Patients in the U.K. You may like to read it... www.leafly.com/news/health - the article is situated on the health page.

The good news is that many medical professionals are starting to listen to their patients and some are even eager to consider – if they are not already – prescribing marijuana as a medical treatment. The amount of information you can receive from your medical professional will depend on where you live and how liberal your doctor is about this subject. If you are wise you will acquire the correct marijuana, while becoming involved in a campaign – on-line – to report on the many benefits medical marijuana brings to you. You can source places that will send it to you by post on-line.

You may need to carry out some further research – certainly if you are thinking about making cannabis oil for the first time – in regard to which strain of the marijuana substance is going to be the most effective for your malady. You may have had that answer supplied to you during the reading of this small book, alas, space cannot allow for the coverage of all maladies and options of which is the best marijuana to source.

Marijuana is usually taken into the body by inhaling it, via a cigarette roll-up scenario – adding the marijuana to tobacco – before smoking the tobacco and marijuana after being mingled together. Oil can also be added to tobacco if oil based marijuana use is the most effective for you.

In the following chapter we will look at some more little know facts about medical marijuana.

Chapter 6 – Some little Known Facts.

There has been much talk about the effects of excessive use of cannabis over the last few years. The information varies from cannabis use being responsible for psychosis and other mind-altering illnesses, to stories of excess paranoia being present in those who partake long-term. Every issue in life these days – probably due to the amount of on-line info' there is – is *widely* debated and of course you have to decide for yourself how you live your life. It is always good to hear the alternative view of any growing concerns about the overuse of cannabis. How many times have you heard of someone being admitted to hospital after a marijuana overdose? I would suggest, none. Compared to the socially accepted drug, alcohol – which accounts for myriad crimes and medical emergencies, every single day – marijuana remains safer and less volatile. In fact it is safer – if judged by the contents of every emergency room in the country – than any other substance one could name that is used in the treatment of acute and chronic illnesses. It has been estimated by independent researchers that it would probably take in the region of 1,000 pounds plus – in weight - of consumed marijuana within *a very small unit of time*, before it resulted in a volatile physical response.

I am certainly not medically trained and so I could not guarantee that smoking marijuana – in excess – would not have some lasting effects upon the brain. The simple answer is that if you are controlling your intake of marijuana for medical purposes, you are less likely to develop any complaint that needs to be treated by a medical professional, than if you were to drink only a moderate amount of alcohol **every day**. The body – mainly the liver and the stomach – needs time to recover from alcohol intake, or they both go into decline very quickly. Marijuana intake of many strains of cannabis – as described in this book – allow the brain to absorb cannabinoids that have been proved to produce a neurogenesis effect – meaning that they help with cell regeneration within the part of the brain that is responsible for mood – and mood disorders. The part of the brain that is benefiting from medical marijuana – the hippocampus - intake will be wholly satisfied with the fact that you are only smoking marijuana. I know what I would want to do if I were suffering from a potentially – in some cases obviously *definitely* – lethal disease and my options were to smoke a substance that helped with the pain, the weight loss and the nausea.

Maybe the biggest debate of all is whether we can convince the researchers that the cannabis plant isn't just a *hit and miss* herbal remedy. There seems to be an incredible amount of professional snobbery concerning substances that are not produced within a laboratory. There was a time however – approximately 1 hundred years, from the mid 1850's, to about the same time one hundred years later – when the U.S.A. pharmaceutical companies **listed** marijuana as one of the most useful medicines for the relief of conditions such as nausea, inflammation of the joints – we now call this rheumatism - and even they even suggested that women in labor should take it to gain pain relief. To add further clarity to the legitimate use of marijuana, it is a historically recorded fact that the first use of the drug for medical purposes occurred in approximately 2800 BCE. It was recorded as being used by the Chinese who celebrated the drug, as a remedy for rheumatism and even gout – although I doubt that the Chinese called it gout. Despite the fact that it may not have been labeled gout, the Chinese knew it hurt and they also knew how to gain relief.

Conclusion

I am convinced that this small book will have – at the very least – provoked a willingness within you to try and gain the best possible relief for whatever malady you are suffering from. The fact is hard to disguise that many people have discovered – or have known for years – that marijuana can be used for medical purposes. We have furnished you with a guide to be able to ensure that you can at least start your quest to find relief, especially if you suffer from any of the following:

Cancer – Treatments for many *symptoms* of cancer can be effectively tackled with the use of medical marijuana. It will never claim to be a cure, but it sure helps with the painful journey.

A.I.D.S. - Any ailment connected with the diagnosis of A.I.D.S including painful conditions that have been brought on by the disease, or are as a result of the contraction of the full-blown, immune lowering – often-fatal – malady, can be eased with medical marijuana.

Epilepsy – The potential to reduce the risk of seizures has to be reason enough to explore the possibility that you may find some relief.

Tourette Syndrome – If the experts cannot find a cure, I know where I would be looking for relief.

Pain – Those with, general muscular, neurological, or nerve damaged induced pain can find hope.

Nausea – Chronic nausea can be a daily agony attached to many diagnosis sheets. It is debilitating and extremely uncomfortable, but there is a remedy.

There are many conditions medical marijuana has been reported to help that I have not had space to investigate –e.g. glaucoma, multiple sclerosis – and so, if you are sufferer of these conditions please seek information regarding medical marijuana. If you suffer from any ailment that has not been mentioned here, you could also investigate whether medical marijuana would help.

My last words go out to all who suffer, especially those who suffer unnecessarily harshly. If you do, seek help, seek information about the benefits you could yield from **medical marijuana.**

Thank you and be well!
Monica.

CPSIA information can be obtained
at www.ICGtesting.com
Printed in the USA
LVHW081524140119
603842LV00020B/1044/P

9 781548 875114